With a rare combination of boldness, wisdom, humility, and grace, Dr. Filby reminds us that the same Spirit who raised Jesus from the dead lives in us and is always ready to work in and through us. You won't find trite formulas here but an invitation to a lifelong journey of learning how to listen to the Spirit's voice, discern where he is moving, and exercise your faith in the adventure of livestreaming with him.

—Bishop Keith Cowart
Free Methodist Church (USA)

Livestream is a wonderful teaching tool for walking a miraculous lifestyle with the Holy Spirit. This will be a great addition to encourage others to live in expectation and readiness to follow the Spirit's leading for an exciting adventure with him!

—Alan Bushell
Director for Youth with a Mission
Saint Augustine, FL (USA)

Livestream will inspire, challenge, and stir up faith and a hunger for ministering in and with the Holy Spirit. It's about being available and responding to God's leading to step out in faith by exercising spiritual gifts. Dr. Filby's amazing testimonies and guided reflections instill confidence and motivates us to venture further into a life of faith adventures.

—Dr. Jeannie Trudel
President of Christian Heritage College
Brisbane, Australia

There is an undeniable winsomeness to Ivan Filby. He is everything you don't expect in a scholar and university president. The Holy Spirit flows from his being and floods these pages. Be healed. Be encouraged. Be equipped.

—Rev. Shane L. Bishop
Sr. Pastor of Christ Church
2010 Distinguished Evangelist of the
United Methodist Church
Fairview Heights, IL (USA)

Livestream by Ivan Filby is an honest, easy to read, practical book that is rooted in Scripture. It is packed with life-giving stories that reveal the power of the Holy Spirit's gifts at work in the lives of ordinary people. I highly recommend it.

—John Townley
National Leader of the
Free Methodist Church in the UK & Ireland
Bristol, England, UK

In this book, Dr. Ivan Filby presents a uniquely dynamic yet down-to-earth journey with the Holy Spirit. With the unreserved sharing of his encounters with the Holy Spirit, Dr. Filby invites us to join him to experience a livestreaming of how God accompanies him in a miraculous way, enabling us to recognize the work of the Holy Spirit whenever and wherever we are in need. This book is an essential tool to increase our spiritual sensitivity and a must-read for every Christian!

—Andrew Yuen
Founder and General Secretary
of the Media Evangelism Ltd. & Creation TV
Hong Kong

Through a narrative that relates powerful testimonies of faith and healing, Ivan Filby guides us to find ways to encounter the Holy Spirit and participate in God's redemptive ministry. Practical while also inspiring, *Livestream* is a welcome resource for anyone who wants to deepen their faith and have their eyes opened to see the miracles that are occurring all around us every day.

—D. Michael Lindsay
President, Taylor University
Upland, IN (USA)

I had the privilege of meeting Ivan Filby many years ago and I saw he had a great gift from the Lord. I love the spirit of this man! There is no doubt that the Lord has given Ivan the freedom to minister to so many that need a touch from the Lord. Ivan's teaching gifting, his ability to reach into the Word of God, is masterly. He has really shown that he is a man who knows the Holy Spirit personally. When I was reading this book, the presence of the Holy Spirit filled my room. You'll be delighted when you also feel the presence of the Holy Spirit reading this book.

—John Steele
Apostolic, Prophetic Gifting
Auckland, New Zealand

Nothing is more encouraging than true stories of God's transforming love delivered with wisdom and insight into how any person can bring that supernatural grace to others. As longtime pastors and founders of a national prayer ministry movement, we prayed this warm book would be read by thousands from the moment we enjoyed the first draft. We've never read a clearer invitation into the hands-on miracle ministry of Jesus than this one that comes from the heart of a couple who live this ministry life credibly and consistently. Our only regret? The book ended.

—**Doug and Margie Newton**

Cofounders of the National Prayer Ministry,
Free Methodist Church US
Milwaukee, WI (USA)

Ivan clearly recognizes the need for the church and communities to have a fresh encounter with the Holy Spirit. Only a renewed emphasis on the ministry and power of the Spirit will enable the church to emerge effectively in the world. I long for this outpouring to be received by all those who read this book.

—**Rev. Ashley Cooper**

Principal Cliff College
Derbyshire UK

Dr. Filby reveals his secret to livestreaming the Holy Spirit in daily life, practically, powerfully, and purposely. He reminds us that being used by the Holy Spirit involves stepping forward in faith, learning, and practicing. The valuable techniques he teaches are ones I am excited about deploying in my own life immediately.

—**Ambassador Kyle McCarter**

USA Marafiki, Kenya
Aid-Trade-Self Reliance

In this book, Dr. Ivan Filby's deep love of Christ and his healing power shines through. Dr. Filby encourages Christians to courageously step away from the safety of the shore and go out onto the water, trusting the Spirit with the outcome.

Serving as both a personal narrative and apologetic, the reader will discover a passionate and heart-stirring theology embedded in the very nature of God through the Holy Spirit.

—**Suzanne Allison Davis**
President, Greenville University, IL (USA)

I am so amazed to read the stories about how Dr. Ivan Filby has experienced the power and the wonders of the Holy Spirit. God is so real. You will be inspired by these true stories and ask God to use you in similar ways. Honestly, I am sure that you will regret it if you miss this book.

—**Rev. David Yip, DMin, PhD**
Senior Pastor
Joyful Praise Assembly, Hong Kong

Dr. Ivan Filby gives practical yet meaningful wisdom for living a dynamic Spirit-led lifestyle. His stories inspire you. His biblical insight will shape you. *Livestream* is great for churches who desire to lean into the supernatural in a balanced way.

—**Pastor Brian V. Warth**
Chapel of Change Christian Fellowship
Los Angeles, CA (USA)

If you are hungry to learn to trust the Holy Spirit and walk in daily obedience to him, and be a conduit of God's healing and power, then *Livestream* is for you. Ivan Filby plainly, simply, and beautifully demonstrates the power of love and mercy that can flow from Spirit-filled believers. You'll be changed by this book!

—**Brett Heintzman**
Director of Communications
Free Methodist Church—USA

Ivan Filby is one of the most compassionate Christian men I have ever met. His work at Greenville University was amazing. Ivan has the rare ability to always place God first in his life and this book illustrates his passion for the Lord.

—Frank Cusumano
Sports Director, KSDK
St. Louis, MO (USA)

Ivan writes with refreshing simplicity on a subject that is controversial and often misunderstood. He communicates with a style that is very practical and subsequently easy to digest. His handling of a deep topic is sufficiently challenging for the experienced and yet simple enough for those new to the conversation. *Livestream* is an excellent articulation well worthy of your consideration

—Scotty Kessler
Director, Robert Coleman School of Discipleship
Director, Wes Neal School of Sports Ministry
Faith International University and Seminary
Tacoma, WA (USA)

Dr. Ivan Filby's writing reflects his heart—a heart fully open to God's voice, a heart reflecting a humble man fully submitting to God's call, and a heart quick to encourage and mentor. Ivan is an exemplar of one ready and willing to take the next faith adventure to which God may call him and in which the Holy Spirit may use him. In *Livestream*, Ivan takes us on a journey in faith adventures each of which is a reminder of God's presence and the movement of the Holy Spirit in our lives.

—Dr. David King
President Malone University
Canton, OH (USA)

I've had the privilege of knowing Ivan for more than twenty-five years and he's one of those unusual individuals that not only gushes out the life of God's Spirit but also is an accomplished and engaging academic. You seldom find this rare combination! His book demonstrates smarts and spirit and is a call to encounter and express God through his Spirit and gifts.

—Kyle Holland

Pastor, Cornerstone Church, Bray, Ireland
Horizon Family of Churches
Church Planter

Dr. Filby masterfully shares how ordinary people are used extraordinarily when led by the Holy Spirit. I highly recommend this book for people of all ages desirous of being used mightily by God.

—Most Reverend Will Boyd, MBA, PhD, PsyD, DD

Patriarch and Chief Servant
Zion Ministries International
Alabama (USA)

Livestream is an apt title and a timely, yet unusual reflection on the work of the Holy Spirit in our lives. It certainly challenged me to ask: *Yes, we are inseparably connected to the Holy Spirt, but how much bandwidth do I allow him in my life?* I would very much like to be a channel of the Spirit's blessing to those around me, but as Dr. Filby asks, Am I willing to give up control? Be vulnerable? Timely and searching questions from a man truly after God's heart.

—Nathan Andrews

Development Consultant and Vice Chair CBMC Asia
Mumbai, India

Ivan Filby has written the most wonderful little book about livestreaming the gifts of the Holy Spirit. I's full of useful exercises and encouraging stories. Get ready to livestream!

—Dr. Miriam O'Regan
Founder, Fearless Women Ireland
Avoca, Co. Wicklow
Republic of Ireland

livestream

LEARNING TO MINISTER IN
THE POWER OF THE HOLY SPIRIT

livestream

IVAN FILBY

Foreword by J. D. Walt

 Seedbed

Scripture quotations are taken from the Holy Bible, New International Version®,
NIV® Copyright © 1973, 1978, 1984, 2011 by Biblica, Inc.™ Used by permission
of Zondervan. All rights reserved worldwide. www.zondervan.com The "NIV"
and "New International Version" are trademarks registered in the United States
Patent and Trademark Office by Biblica, Inc.™ All rights reserved worldwide.

Printed in the United States of America

Cover design by Strange Last Name
Page design by PerfecType, Nashville, Tennessee

Filby, Ivan, 1962-
  Livestream : learning to minister in the power of the Holy Spirit / Ivan Filby. –
Franklin, Tennessee : Seedbed Publishing, ©2021.

   pages ; cm .

   ISBN 9781628248975 (paperback)
   ISBN 9781628248982 (Mobi)
   ISBN 9781628248999 (ePub)
   ISBN 9781628249002 (uPDF)
   OCLC 1260366887

   1. Gifts, Spiritual. 2. Pastoral theology. 3. Holy Spirit. I. Title.

BT767.3.F55 2021   234.13   2021943207

 Seedbed

SEEDBED PUBLISHING
Franklin, Tennessee
seedbed.com

To Kathie, Sam, and Katie

Contents

Foreword

There is a simple and yet comprehensive text that over-arches and undergirds the book before us. Hear the words of Jesus Messiah: "My Father is always at his work to this very day, and I too am working" (John 5:17).

There are many books which purport to tell others how to do the work of God. This is not one of those books. This book shares with us what it means and looks like to participate in the working of God. The distinction may seem subtle. It is not.

Jesus further clarifies his point two verses later: "Very truly I tell you, the Son can do nothing by himself; he can do only what he sees his Father doing, because whatever the Father does the Son also does" (v. 19).

This is the essence of the concept of *livestreaming*, the whole point of this book. Jesus goes on: "For the Father loves the Son and shows him all he does. Yes, and he will show him even greater works than these, so that you will be amazed" (v. 20).

Now, let's complete the logic and close the loop. Go with me to Jesus' final discourse to his disciples in John's Gospel: "Very truly I tell you, whoever believes in me will do the works I have been doing, and they will do even greater things than these, because I am going to the Father" (John 14:12).

The point and purpose of this book is not to teach us the functional techniques of how to do the works of God as though we could somehow learn the method. No, this book aspires to call us to live in a transcendent, transformational union with the Son of God through the gift of his Spirit—for our good, for others' gain, and for God's glory.

I first began to hear about Ivan Filby through a steady stream of students coming from Greenville College to study at Asbury Seminary, where I served as dean of the chapel. They described him as a professor who had deeply invested in and impacted their lives. From their stories I pictured him as a kind of Jedi Knight, a man who moved in the power of the Holy Spirit who had a cool British accent.

I commented about how great it was when a Bible or theology professor brought this kind of experience and anointing to their teaching. That's when they told me he was not in the religion department at all—he was a professor in the business department. Now I was really intrigued. Though I despise the term, Ivan Filby is a layperson. I much prefer the term *player*. Borrowing the terminology of the late John Wimber, founder of the Vineyard Church, Ivan Filby was doing "the stuff" Jesus did.

I think Jesus is always glad when the coaching staff can do "the stuff" he did, but he is particularly pleased when the everyday players on the team—the ones he called "my church"—move and minister in the power of the Holy Spirit. That's the Ivan Filby I've been hearing about for the past twenty years, the author of this long-awaited work, *Livestream*.

Speaking of the title, he is generous to credit me with the livestreaming metaphor. The Holy Spirit is the third person of the Trinity, the outpoured livestreaming presence of the living God in and through human beings. The Holy Spirit brings the living, active presence of Jesus Christ to us and through us to others.

I don't know about you, but I am far more comfortable with a download than a livestream. With a download, I am in control. I can play it on demand, fast-forwarding, rewinding, pausing, and stopping as I wish. I don't need a cell signal or even Wi-Fi. With a livestream, I am dependent on a strong signal. Nothing is more frustrating than dealing with all the buffering interruptions when trying to watch a video online with a weak signal. As I understand him, the Holy Spirit cannot be downloaded, only livestreamed. We do not possess God. God possesses us.

Here's how I hear Jesus saying it: "Abide in me as I abide in you. No branch can bear fruit by itself, it must abide in the vine. Neither can you bear fruit unless you abide in me"

(John 15:4, paraphrased). That's livestreaming. It's not a perfect metaphor, but you get the point.

Ivan Filby takes the metaphor to the next level in the pages that follow. Through Scripture and story, he weaves one example after another, showing us how the Holy Spirit brings the gifts of grace into the lives of ordinary people in everyday situations. As Jesus was on earth, so he is in heaven, and as he is in heaven, so we are on earth. As Jesus only did what he saw his Father doing, so he intends the same for us. As Jesus ministered powerfully in the streaming love of the Holy Spirit, so he intends the same for us.

Be warned. Though filled with helpful guidance, this is not a step-by-step guide to mastering ministry in the livestreaming power of the Holy Spirit. It is the wisdom, witness, and testimony of a man of God who has walked with Jesus for many years. Ivan and Kathie Filby are the real deal. It is my privilege to commend this inspiring work to the church.

> "My Father is always at his work to this very day, and I too am working." (John 5:17)

It is time for us to join his working. It is time to move on from the lesser things and lay hold of the greater things. Jesus awaits.

For the Awakening
John David (J. D.) Walt Jr.
Pentecost 2021

Acknowledgments

I have many people to thank. Here's just a few of them:

First, the board of trustees gifted me with a sabbatical at the end of my term as president of Greenville University. Their gift of time enabled me to write the first draft of this book.

I'm grateful to the men who took the time to mentor me, including Mark Habgood, John Steele, and Doug Newton, as well as men who are now with the Lord, including Frank Hultgren and Geoff Shipman.

Megan Hall, Doug and Margie Newton, and Linda Myette all read various sections of the manuscript and offered insightful feedback.

I'm thankful to the dedicated people at Seedbed Publishing, particularly J. D. Walt for inspiring us through the Daily Text. Also, thanks to Andrew Dragos and Andrew Miller for suggesting ways to tighten up the manuscript.

Most of all, I'm thankful to my wife, Kathie, who not only read every word of this manuscript but partnered with me throughout these adventures.

Soli Deo Gloria.

ONE

livestreaming

"Which of you fathers, if your son asks for a fish, will give him a snake instead? Or if he asks for an egg, will give him a scorpion? If you then, though you are evil, know how to give good gifts to your children, how much more will your Father in heaven give the Holy Spirit to those who ask him!"

—Luke 11:11–13

I walked from my seat to the microphone at the front of the church.

"I keep getting this impression there's someone here whose hands keep getting hot and cold and are very painful. I've no idea what the condition is, but I think God wants to heal you."

1

I looked out at the Parkview Free Methodist Church's congregation to see who might respond.

"That's me," came a booming voice from behind. "I think that's me."

I turned around. Dennis, the bass player, continued, "I have Raynaud's syndrome. My hands are cold, and my fingers are very white, sometimes blueish. They are either numb or painful, one or the other. I've lost feeling in my toes, too, and they hurt if it's cold outside."

"Can we pray for you?" I asked.

Pastor John Glennon joined me at the front of the sanctuary. We laid hands on Dennis.

"Father, in the name of Jesus, I take authority over Raynaud's syndrome. We command it to leave. Father, let warmth and feeling come back into Dennis's fingers and toes."

I asked Dennis to let me know if he experienced any change. Two days later, he sent me a text.

"This is Dennis. I wanted to let you know I have experienced healing from Raynaud's syndrome in the past couple of days. I'll give you more details when I see you."

I couldn't wait. I asked for more details then and there.

"The numbness has nearly all disappeared, and I've regained feeling in my toes. Also, warmth has mostly returned to my extremities."

Dennis sent me another update three days later. "Feet okay. Gone is the numbness I felt every morning. My fingers are a bit cold but are pink in color in that I have blood flow. They would go white during an episode and difficult to warm up. Not so now, thankfully."

I asked Dennis for an update three years later, as I was writing his story. He texted: "I continue to do well, thank the Lord. No problems with hands at all."

When I set out on the twenty-minute drive from the president's house at Greenville University to Parkview Free Methodist Church in Vandalia, Illinois, on Sunday, November 5, 2017, I had no idea God was about to heal Dennis. It wasn't until the Holy Spirit livestreamed the impression that he wanted to heal a person with painful hands that I knew anything about it at all. This was a Holy Spirit–initiated ministry opportunity from start to finish. When I initiate ministry, not much happens. However, when the Holy Spirit takes the lead, all things are possible when we follow along.

Over the last forty years, I've followed the Holy Spirit into literally hundreds of these faith adventures, and I've included a few of them in this book. Although I have changed a person's name here and there to preserve their privacy, all the stories are true. While these real encounters will encourage every reader, I've selected these stories with three groups of people in mind. First, I meet many people who hunger for a more profound experience with the Holy Spirit but just don't know where to begin. If this is you, I hope this book will give you the confidence to step out. Next, some of you have experienced the

Holy Spirit working through you occasionally, but you've not yet learned to flow in the gifts naturally. I hope I can encourage you too. Finally, there will be readers who are used regularly by the Holy Spirit. You'll find plenty of stories in this book that resonate with your own experience and whet your appetite for more. Most important, I hope the book inspires you to mentor others. I meet countless folk eager to begin their adventure with the Holy Spirit. I meet far fewer mentors. I pray that this book encourages you to start or continue to mentor those you meet.

I should say at the outset that I still have much to learn. Compared to some, I'm still a novice. Compared to others, I'm like a Jedi Master of the Spirit. Regardless of our level of maturity or need for development, our responsibility is to keep in step with the Holy Spirit, grow in our use of spiritual gifts, and pass along what we have learned to others. There is always much more to learn, and still people we can mentor. We grow best when we humbly learn from those more experienced than us and serve those following behind.

Charisma

I find it remarkable that I didn't hear much about the Holy Spirit during my first two years as a Jesus follower, especially when the apostle Paul goes to some length to instruct the church in the appropriate use of spiritual gifts. In 1 Corinthians 12:1, Paul wrote: "Now about the gifts of the Spirit, brothers and sisters, I do not want you to be uninformed." Paul listed nine of the Holy Spirit's gifts later in this chapter:

> Now to each one the manifestation of the Spirit is given for the common good. To one there is given through the Spirit a message of wisdom, to another a message of knowledge by means of the same Spirit, to another faith by the same Spirit, to another gifts of healing by that one Spirit, to another miraculous powers, to another prophecy, to another distinguishing between spirits, to another speaking in different kinds of tongues, and to still another the interpretation of tongues. All these are the work of one and the same Spirit, and he distributes them to each one, just as he determines. (vv. 7–11)

The Greek word Paul uses for "gift" is *charisma*, from which we get the term "charismatic gifts." *Charis* means "grace" while *charisma* means "grace-gifts." In more common vernacular, charisma, or charismatic gifts, are Holy Spirit–empowered gifts enabling a Jesus follower to share in God's work for the good of others. The emphasis on grace is important. We cannot earn these gifts; Father God freely gives them to us for the benefit of others. They are not a sign of maturity but, rather, availability.

I've often heard folk talk about the nine gifts of the Holy Spirit. While it is true that Paul listed nine in his letter to the Corinthian church, he added six more—serving, teaching, encouraging, giving, leading, and mercy—in his letter to Jesus followers in Rome:

> We have different gifts, according to the grace given to each of us. If your gift is prophesying, then prophesy in accordance with your faith; if it is serving, then serve; if it is teaching, then teach; if it is to encourage, then give encouragement; if it is giving, then give generously; if it is to lead, do it diligently; if it is to show mercy, do it cheerfully. (Rom. 12:6–8)

Between these two passages, Paul listed fifteen charismatic gifts. I know people who are very passionate about which gifts should be included or omitted from this list. I don't find these arguments helpful. After all, the Holy Spirit's gifts are not like some holy Cub Scout badges we try to collect, showing how smart or good we are. The gifts don't even give us a set of stripes advancing us through the ranks from a spiritual private to a corporal, sergeant, lieutenant, or captain. Instead, the gifts enable us to serve others in a way that we never could without the Holy Spirit's empowerment. I'd rather spend my time pursuing the Holy Spirit than fighting over a definitive list. Where's the fun in that?

What Paul Didn't Say

The context of Paul's letter is vital. Corinth was a pagan city, full of immorality, idolatry, and divisiveness. Paul was not writing to a church that had no exposure to the use of the gifts of the Holy Spirit. Rather, he wrote to a church that did not use the gifts for the common good (see 1 Corinthians 12:8). The Corinthians were immature in their use of spiritual gifts. From Paul's letter, we can glean that the Corinthians likely used spiritual gifts in a free-for-all, no-holds-barred, anything-goes approach. They were not ignorant about the Holy Spirit's gifts per se; they were uninformed about how to use the gifts well.

The Corinthian church faced many serious issues that Paul addressed in his letter to the Corinthian church: sexual immorality, a lack of love among Jesus followers, a lack of order when celebrating Communion, and a lack of wisdom using these spiritual gifts. Interestingly, Paul never doubted that these gifts are from the Holy Spirit, and that's important. Given the Corinthian church's immature use of spiritual gifts, not to mention the church's moral failings, he might have questioned the validity of gifts or told the church to quit livestreaming until their lives were more ordered. I can imagine Paul writing: "Now listen up, you Corinthians. You are no longer allowed to speak in tongues or prophesy until you get your lives in order. You're a disgrace to us all. You need to grow up. Stop using spiritual gifts until you learn to use them responsibly. That's an order!"

I find it intriguing that Paul didn't take this approach. Instead, he wrote: "Follow the way of love and eagerly desire gifts of the Spirit, especially prophecy" (1 Cor. 14:1).

What Paul Did Say

Instead of discouraging the use of spiritual gifts, he encouraged the Corinthians to desire them even more. Why? Because a mature use of the Holy Spirit's gifts is vital for the healthy growth of any church. We should not be surprised to learn that most churches multiplying worldwide are very open to the use of spiritual gifts. Paul knew that the gifts of the Holy Spirit were not the real problem in the Corinthian church. Instead, immaturity, immorality, and the lack of proper teaching were at the root of the church's problems.

Paul's letter was probably the first time the Corinthian church had heard any instructions on the mature and orderly use of spiritual gifts so that everyone could benefit. Helpfully, Paul gave the Corinthian church extensive advice to help them use spiritual gifts well. We do well to keep these in mind:

- Don't be ignorant about spiritual gifts. (1 Cor. 12:1)
- There are different types of gifts and ministries, and all of them are needed for the church to function well. (12:7–11)
- God gives different spiritual gifts as he deems fit. (12:11)
- Spiritual gifts are intended for the common good, not to make you look good. (12:7, 21–25)
- Speaking in tongues might be talking in human or angelic languages. (13:1)

- Unless our motivation is love, using spiritual gifts gains us nothing. (13:1–3)
- Even the most gifted of us only see or know part of the picture. Stay humble. (13:9–11)
- If anyone speaks a public message in tongues, they should also pray for the interpretation so everyone can benefit. (13:13)
- Eagerly desire spiritual gifts; they help build the church. (14:1)
- Speaking in tongues is speaking mysteries by the Spirit. Only God understands it. (14:2)
- Those who speak in tongues don't talk to people but talk to God. (14:2)
- The person who prophesies speaks to people for their encouragement, strengthening, and comfort. (14:3)
- Prophecy is a better gift for public worship. (14:5)
- Be eager to use spiritual gifts that build up other people. (14:12)
- When a person prays in tongues, their spirit prays, but their mind has no idea what's going on. (14:14)
- It's beneficial to pray both in tongues and your natural human language. (14:15)
- It's great to speak in tongues, but in church, it is preferable to speak words that others can understand so they can be strengthened. (14:19)

- When the church comes together, everyone has a part to play. (14:26)
- Up to three people may prophesy at one time, and others must carefully weigh what is said. (14:29)
- You are responsible for using spiritual gifts in an orderly way. (14:32–33)
- Be eager to prophesy. (14:39)
- Don't forbid speaking in tongues. (14:39)
- Do everything in an orderly way to build up other people's faith. (14:40)

Not everyone takes advice well. Some people are know-it-alls who don't seek anyone's help. Sadly, church history has had far too many such men and women. Thankfully, the Corinthians were not among them. How do we know? Paul writes to them again in 2 Corinthians and doesn't see the need to bring up the issue again. The Corinthians appear to have taken correction well. We would do well to emulate the Corinthian church, not in their sensuality, but in their willingness to put things right.

Livestreaming

I recently heard speaker and author J. D. Walt differentiate between downloading and livestreaming in the Christian life. He likened downloading to preparing a sermon. A sermon is researched, rehearsed, and delivered at a set time and place.

A person preparing a talk or sermon knows what they want to say and (hopefully) how to bring the address to a close. Livestreaming is the exact opposite. It is spontaneous, unrehearsed, and can happen anywhere and at any time of the Holy Spirit's choosing.

I find livestreaming a helpful metaphor, and I'll use it throughout the book to capture the sense of risk and excitement of allowing the Holy Spirit to move in and through us. We simply have no idea what the Holy Spirit will do next. When we stream the Holy Spirit's love and power, we live a life full of jaw-dropping, head-scratching, mind-boggling surprises.

Throughout the book, you'll find livestreaming stories interwoven with thoughtful reflection. This interlacing of real stories with insight replicates how livestreaming works in practice. Allowing the Holy Spirit to livestream through us is always an act of faith and often leads us into new experiences. As we reflect upon our livestreaming experiences, our questions naturally lead us to pray for insight, search Scripture for wisdom, and learn from others as we seek to make sense of what the Lord has done. In turn, when we pray and study, it's like we are holding up our hand, asking the Holy Spirit to "pick me, pick me" when he wants to livestream again. And so on!

The tremendous privilege we have as Jesus followers is that we get to help one another along on our journeys of faith. Spiritual gifts, used well, are tools in God's arsenal that he uses to shape us into his image. That's why God so passionately wants to livestream the Holy Spirit's gifts through us. Not for entertainment, nor to make anyone look good, and certainly not to facilitate any form of spiritual manipulation or skulduggery, but so that we can help one another become like Jesus. We can't do this in isolation. We desperately need others to speak into our lives, just as others will need our encouragement and support along the way.

Spot the Gift: Case Study

When we livestream the Holy Spirit's gifts, we don't focus on any individual spiritual gift. Instead, we seek to be open to any gift the Holy Spirit wants to stream through us according to the need of the moment, whether that be prophecy, encouragement, healing, words of wisdom, giving, leadership, or faith. Often what's needed is a combination of several. The good news is that we don't have to figure it out; the Holy Spirit is well able to do that. Our job is to accept his invitation for adventure and jump on board the faith bus.

See if you can spot the spiritual gifts used in the following story. You'll quickly find the gifts of giving, healing, and miracles. Less obvious are the gifts of wisdom, faith, and encouragement. As you read, count how many gifts were used in a church setting.

"Ya Gotta Know Who Your Daddy Is!"

One of my responsibilities as president of Greenville University was to raise scholarship dollars for our students. I was always eager to share my vision for the university with like-minded folk who had a passion for Jesus Christ and philanthropic hearts. A friend suggested I call Bob, one of his buddies. I learned that Bob was a deeply committed Jesus follower with a big wallet and a generous heart. The university wanted to establish some new scholarship programs, and I'd hoped Bob would consider making a significant gift to endow one of these scholarships. I was eager to contact him and hopefully set up a time to meet.

After several attempts to reach each other by phone, Bob and I finally connected. I introduced him to my work at Greenville University and told him a little about my experiences following Jesus. Bob told me his story. He was the top salesperson in the nation for a leading company at one point in his life, making a six-figure income each year in commission alone. Like many successful people, Bob decided to start his own business. He resigned from his job, set up his own company, and began to advertise his services. Things did not start well. The first year of business was a disaster. Even though he worked harder than ever, he brought home only $11,000 instead of the six-figure sum he'd expected. Things got so bad he thought he might lose his car, his house, everything.

As Bob contemplated financial ruin, he became desperate. So desperate that he began to spend more and more time in prayer. He told me he began to have, and I quote, "stellar quiet times." Every day Bob read the Bible for an hour, prayed for fifteen minutes, and then sat quietly, learning to listen to God. Bob told me that nothing happened at first, but after a while, it felt like God started to livestream ideas into his head to help him grow his business. He wrote these ideas down, figured out how to add them to his business, and started doing them. His business grew and grew some more. After a while, he became so successful that significant competitors began to take notice. One of them offered to buy Bob's business for $100 million.

After selling his business, Bob continued to have extended times of prayer. During one of these prayer times, God told him to give away a considerable proportion of the money he earned from the sale. He put together a plan to give away millions and millions of dollars over the next five years.

I've never met anyone who gets so excited about giving money away. Bob kept quoting Matthew 6:19–21 to me:

"Do not store up for yourselves treasures on earth, where moths and vermin destroy, and where thieves break in and steal. But store up for yourselves treasures in heaven, where moths and vermin do not destroy, and where thieves do not break in and steal. For where your treasure is, there your heart will be also."

After our fourth or fifth call, Bob began to confide in me. Bob told me that he and his wife, Amanda, wanted to start a family but could not conceive. Bob said to me that every month, when it was apparent that Amanda wasn't pregnant, it was very hard for them, especially for Amanda. He asked me to pray for them.

To encourage him, I told Bob about Meg and Joe, two of my friends from Ireland. Meg and Joe had been married for several years but were unable to conceive. During tests for in vitro fertilization, the doctors discovered they had a rare condition in which her cervical mucus's biochemistry destroyed his sperm; it was medically impossible for them to conceive. During one of my many trips from Dublin to the United States, I met with a pastor from Atlanta who told me there was a group of women in his church who had successfully prayed for eight infertile couples, all of whom now had children. I asked the pastor if this group of women would be willing to pray with Meg and Joe. He assured me the women would love the faith challenge. Meg and Joe flew to Atlanta for a couple of weeks, and the women prayed with them every day. Six months later, Meg conceived, and they had a beautiful baby girl.

I tried to locate the contact information for this pastor and church but couldn't. I searched through my files and social media but couldn't find either the pastor or the church. When

I called Bob to tell him I'd reached a dead end trying to connect him with the pastor, I could hear the sadness in his voice.

I added Bob to my prayer calendar, and I told him that I'd swing by to pray with them if I were ever in his area. When I found out my travels would take me close to his city, I gave Bob a call to see if they'd be able to join us for dinner.

We found the restaurant with no problem, arriving a few minutes early. I hadn't seen a photo of Bob or Amanda, but as soon as I saw this guy walk into the restaurant with an enormous grin, I knew it had to be them. We hugged and chatted away like we'd been lifelong friends.

I shared a little about our experience with the Holy Spirit. I've found that telling stories about God's goodness creates faith naturally. We found out Bob and Amanda were no strangers to healing. Bob told us he had recently returned from a trip to Israel. One day during his tour, the bus driver parked near one of the locations where Jesus had performed miracles. The driver read a few passages of Scripture, turned around to face his passengers, and told them, "Jesus still heals today." The driver offered to pray for anyone on the bus. To Bob's surprise, one of his buddies went forward for prayer. Many years ago, his friend had been recruited to play NCAA Division One football for a major US university but was injured in his freshman year. He never got to play and suffered many years of pain. His friend made his way to the front of the bus, and the driver prayed for him. He later told Bob that he felt heat shoot down his body when the bus driver prayed for him. He was completely healed.

Bob shook his head. "He was a bus driver, Ivan! Not a pastor or a priest, a bus driver!"

The story continued and Bob told us that as his friend walked to the back of the bus, he sat down next to Bob and told him, "Bob, ya gotta know who your daddy is!"

Bob paused, then looked me right in the eye and said, "Ivan, ya gotta know who your daddy is."

Bob's friend was right. The more we understand our heavenly Father, the more we know who our daddy is, the deeper our relationship with God will become.

By the end of our meal, we were the only folks in our section of the restaurant.

"It's been so good to meet you finally, Bob," I said. "And to meet you too, Amanda," I said, turning to face her. "Would you allow Kathie and me to pray with you guys? We'll be discreet. Who knows what God might do? I know he's good."

They both agreed. I asked Amanda and Bob to put their hands over Amanda's abdomen, and Kathie and I placed our hands on top of theirs. Our prayer was short. We cursed a spirit of death and simply asked the Lord to bless them with new life. We said amen, hugged them, and went our separate ways.

Six weeks later, I received an e-mail from Bob. The subject line contained only one word: "Thanks." The attachment was the video file from Amanda's first prenatal scan. She was pregnant.

Spot the Gift: Answers

I'm sure you spotted that Bob had the gift of giving. We saw two healings: Bob's buddy's back and Amanda's healing enabling her to conceive. We saw one miracle: Meg and Joe's underlying biochemical mismatch was not healed, but they did get their miracle baby. Bob received several words of wisdom to grow his business. The women in Atlanta had the gift of faith, and I encouraged Bob. What's also interesting is that none of these Holy Spirit events happened in a church. If you find yourself in a church not supportive of the gifts of the Holy Spirit, no problem; there's plenty of work to do in the marketplace.

How Much More?

When Jesus taught his disciples to pray, he introduced them to the idea of addressing God as Father. This must have astounded their first-century Jewish minds. Jesus went on to describe the type of Father he had in mind. In Luke 11:11–13, Jesus describes the generous heart of God the Father:

> "Which of you fathers, if your son asks for a fish, will give him a snake instead? Or if he asks for an egg, will give him a scorpion? If you then, though you are evil,

know how to give good gifts to your children, how
much more will your Father in heaven give the Holy
Spirit to those who ask him!"

Jesus describes his heavenly Father as generous, longing to
give good gifts and giving the Holy Spirit. The problem is not
on God's side. He's on the edge of his seat, ready, willing, and
able to bless us, just waiting for us to ask.

Have you ever been excited to give a gift to someone?
Perhaps a Christmas gift for a family member that you spent
time researching, saving for, carefully wrapping. Or a gift for
your first boyfriend or girlfriend, an engagement ring, a gift
for your first grandchild, or a "just because" gift to a special
friend. Can you remember how exciting it was to think about
giving the gift? I bet you couldn't even sleep the night before.
God is far more excited to give you the gifts of the Holy
Spirit than you were to give your gift to your friend or family
member. The problem is not that he doesn't want to stream
the Holy Spirit's gifts through us; the problem is that we often
don't know how to receive them.

I understand this frustration. I've felt it many times. I
think this is especially challenging for those who have grown
up in the Western world. Over the last two hundred years, the
Western world has denied the reality of a supernatural world.
Our upbringing leads us to conclude that if we can't see, feel,
touch, taste, or smell something, then it's not real. Or, if we do

believe in a supernatural world, we don't regard it as quite as important or influential as the physical world we can far more easily explain and measure.

A good friend of mine, Christie Kessinger, is currently writing a national children's church curriculum that teaches kids how to listen to the Holy Spirit and follow God. Christie often tells church leaders and parents that God does not give children a "mini Holy Spirit." She makes a valid point. Church leaders and parents sometimes talk as if God does not give children the Holy Spirit's full measure until they are older. I don't see any scriptural evidence for this. In contrast, Jesus repeatedly told his listeners to become like little children again. Why? Because small children find it so much easier to receive than adults. They are more trusting, more imaginative, and love gifts.

As problematic as it is to give the impression that kids only receive a mini Holy Spirit, I think an even bigger problem in the church is that adults often act as if they have somehow been given a watered-down version of the Holy Spirit. In Romans 8:11, the apostle Paul wrote that we have been given the same Spirit that raised Christ from the dead. That's just mind-boggling. The same Spirit that brought a dead man back to life, the same Spirit that opened graves on resurrection morning, and the same Spirit that tore a colossal temple curtain in two from top to bottom lives in us. God wants us to live our lives armed and dangerous, mobilized, and ready to take on evil in the name of Jesus. Sadly, we often settle for a tame religion where all we expect from the Holy Spirit is to give us peace.

Over to You: Goody Bags

When I'm ministering, I often ask people to close their eyes and remember any children's birthday parties they've attended. I invite you to do the same. I'm aware not every kid got invited, and not all who did had a good experience, but most people were invited to a kid's party at one time or another in their lives. I hope you can think of a happy one.

Close your eyes and remember your childhood days. Think about a birthday party you attended. There were gifts for the birthday boy or girl, some games, some food, and a birthday cake with candles. Just as the party was coming to an end, the host parent began to give out goody bags. Their contents vary from place to place and culture to culture, but these little bags perhaps contain a toy, some crayons, a whistle, and some candy. There's a gift bag for every child who attends. The host parent had carefully prepared one for every guest, including you, and likely filled a few extra ones in case of mini gate-crashers!

Every child received a goody bag. No one was left out. If a child had been a perfect guest, she got one. If a child was hyper after eating too much cake, he got one. If a child lost every game, she still got one. You got one too. Getting the bag was not dependent on height, skin color, gender, intellect, neighborhood, language, clothes, or even behavior. Getting the gift bag was simply the result of two things: (1) you were invited to the party and (2) the birthday kid's parent went to a lot of trouble and some expense preparing the bag for you.

Don't think about your own father at this moment, however excellent or imperfect he may have been. Think about God as your Father. He is generous and kind. God wants to stream spiritual gifts through you so that more people experience his deep love.

When the host parent gave us the party bags, all we had to do was receive. In the same way, our heavenly Father has invited you to his party. He has a parting gift. He doesn't want us to leave without it.

Quietly sit so that you could hear a pin drop. But you're not listening for pins; you are listening for the whispers of the Holy One, saying, "I love you; I forgive you; you are mine. Come back; come close; come in."

Simply pray, "Come, Holy Spirit," the first words of the beautiful ancient prayer, "Come, Holy Spirit, fill the hearts of your faithful and enkindle in them the fire of your love."

Now, wait for a minute or two. Perhaps the Lord will bring a Scripture, friend, or incident to your mind. Write down anything that comes to your mind so you can sift through it later. If nothing comes to your mind, don't worry. Remember

Bob prayed for several weeks before he had his first livestream. It will happen because God loves you and wants to use you. It's a promise, not from me, but from the good, good Father.

Questions for Reflection and Conversation

1. When you hear the words *Father God*, what do you imagine God is like? What words would you use to describe God? Are you able to differentiate God's qualities from your own father's?

2. What was the best gift your earthly dad ever gave to you? In the light of this, reflect on Jesus' saying, "If you then, though you are evil, know how to give good gifts to your children, how much more will your Father in heaven give the Holy Spirit to those who ask him!" (Luke 11:13).

3. Think back over your life. Can you spot times when the Holy Spirit has livestreamed through you to bless others?

4. Why do you think Paul gave so many instructions on the use of spiritual gifts?

TWO

cutting remarks

> To one there is given through the Spirit a word
> of wisdom, to another a word of knowledge by
> means of the same Spirit.
>
> —1 Corinthians 12:8

Perhaps you're familiar with the worship song, "Good
Good Father." I wasn't. I was standing in the chapel at
Malone University, preparing to speak to well more than
one thousand students. My wife, Kathie, and I had spent the
weekend in Canton, Ohio, as part of the Christian College
Consortium presidents' group. A couple of months before our
gathering, Malone University's president, Dr. David King,

invited Kathie and me to extend our stay by one day so I could speak in chapel.

To be honest, I was nervous as I climbed the stage to speak. I was comfortable with my material. I'd planned to talk about the goodness of God and the work of the Holy Spirit. However, I was speaking at a university this time. I didn't know if this university chapel was primarily an educational event or whether they might be open to the Holy Spirit's ministry.

After dinner the night before, I had spent an hour or so praying about this chapel service. During this prayer time, the Holy Spirit livestreamed three insights that led me to believe the Lord had something up his sleeve for the following morning's chapel. The Bible calls these insights "words of knowledge," which is one of the Holy Spirit's gifts listed by the apostle Paul in 1 Corinthians 12:7–11.

Quite often, the Holy Spirit wants to do things through us that are impossible for us to do alone. Words of knowledge are simply insights the Lord livestreams to help us minister more effectively. Do you remember Jesus telling his disciples that he only did what he saw the Father doing (see John 5:19)? Words of knowledge are simply one way the Lord shares what he wants to do and invites us to participate.

Words of Knowledge

Words of knowledge come in all shapes and sizes and are often precursors to healing ministry. I know some people supernaturally feel other people's pain. When this happens, the person receiving the word of knowledge can describe very accurately to a congregation, group, or individual the condition they feel. When a person hears their pain described with such accuracy, it raises their level of faith. I know of many people through whom God livestreams this way. I'm just not one of them, more's the pity. Likely, I have too many aches and pains of my own to discern which ache is a word of knowledge and which is just my aging body saying ouch.

From time to time, when I'm preparing for public ministry, the Holy Spirit livestreams a picture or movie clip into my mind's eye. This is a second way people can receive words of knowledge. Sometimes, this movie clip streams only once, and sometimes it loops a couple of times. Sometimes these clips are crystal clear and sharp; at other times, much less so. In many respects, this streaming looks like any other thought that goes through your head. Until someone told me to look out for these livestreams from the Spirit, I'd simply dismissed them as odd ideas floating around in my head. It never dawned on me that the Holy Spirit might be inviting me to join him on a ministry adventure.

During my prayer time the night before chapel, I saw a livestream of a woman pulling up a black cardigan sleeve and cutting her forearm with a razor blade. I couldn't see her face or see anything else about her. One of my late mentors, Australian pastor Frank Hultgren, trained me to look carefully at these pictures and movie clips to make sure I didn't miss important details. As I reviewed the streamed clip, I noticed the woman was holding the blade in her right hand and cutting her left forearm. Her skin was smooth and not wrinkled. I concluded she was a right-handed young woman. Additionally, as I thought about the clip, I felt sure the woman's self-harm resulted from sexual abuse she'd endured during an earlier stage of her life. This information was not part of the movie clip itself. Nonetheless, I knew this to be the case. How? Through a third way the Holy Spirit streams information to us: merely knowing. It wasn't anything I'd thought about or worked out by analysis. Instead, it's instantly knowing something; one second, you know nothing, and the next, the idea is fully formed in your head.

My second word of knowledge was in the form of a still picture. I could see a human neck with a thread running down the right side of the neck. This picture looked more like a diagrammatic medical poster pinned to the doctor's office wall than a real person. All I could see was the neck; I couldn't tell if it was a man or woman. I knew the thread running down the side was causing someone pain. I had no idea if the thread indicated a failed surgery, some demonic activity, or even an injury. I hoped that would become clear during ministry.

My final word of knowledge also came in the form of knowing. While I was praying, I simply became aware that a physician had previously told someone who would attend chapel that one of their legs was shorter than the other. I didn't know if the person was male or female, young or old. I didn't know if a birth abnormality or an accident caused this condition. All I knew was that the unevenness was causing pain.

It's worth noting that words of knowledge can stream in other ways too. A fourth way people can receive words of knowledge is by seeing words written or floating on people, places, or buildings. Sometimes, I see words superimposed over a person's face. I know the words are not physically there, but I see them nonetheless, sometimes very clearly and, at other times, only faintly. I am sure I'd miss many if I hadn't taken the time to look. I might see words like *jaw*, *heart condition*, or *nightmares*. I find these words are a helpful way to begin a conversation to discern better how to pray for the person. The more casual these conversations are, the better. Instead of saying, "God told me such and such," try saying, "As I was praying for you, I wondered if you were having pain in your lower back. I might be wrong, but I wanted to check, just in case you'd like me to pray for you."

A final way of receiving words of knowledge worth mentioning now is by speaking them out. Sometimes, when I'm praying with someone, I pray about things I would have no natural way of knowing. For example, one time, a man asked me to pray about his work situation. During my time of prayer for him, I began praying about deep disappointments the man had experienced as a result of a childhood friend's betrayal. As I prayed, he began to weep. When I started our prayer time, I had no clue at all I'd be praying about a deep-seated disappointment. After we had said our amens, the man told me he hadn't thought about that disappointment for years and was surprised and embarrassed that he had teared up. He'd forgotten, but the Lord had not. God is kind and generous like that. God wants us whole.

Cutting Remarks

As the chapel worship at Malone was coming to an end, I reviewed my message and the three words of knowledge I'd written in the margins of my notes. I wanted to communicate clearly and accurately. The worship certainly helped to create a faith-filled atmosphere.

As I sang "Good Good Father," I was reminded that our ultimate value doesn't rest on our education, looks, or accomplishments. Our value stems from the fact that God loves us. He chooses to love us, knowing all our grubby little secrets and our tendencies to fall short, give up, puff up, run out, or talk down. The more we can grasp this beautiful truth, the easier it is for us to receive from the good, good Father.

The worship team unplugged their equipment and laid down their guitars. The meeting leader introduced me, and I spoke for perhaps twenty-five minutes. I closed with this invitation: "Kathie and I will hang around for a few minutes after chapel. We'd love the opportunity to pray with you. As I was preparing, I got three little nudges I believe are from the Holy Spirit. If you're one of these people, we'd especially love to pray for you."

I described the three conditions I saw in the livestreams—the young woman cutting herself, the neck with the thread running down, and the legs of different lengths.

After praying a blessing over the Malone University faculty, staff, and students, I left the stage and was taken to a side space curtained off from the main auditorium. Kathie and I prayed for several people.

When Nothing Happens

The first person we prayed for was a young woman who had been in a car accident. She told us that even though her legs look the same length, they were not. She had injured her hips in the accident, and one leg was longer than the other. We asked her to sit on a bench. I held her ankles and prayed several times. Nothing happened.

It wasn't a good start. I'd had a word of knowledge, a person had responded, we'd prayed for her several times in front of about twenty other students, and nothing appeared to happen. She neither felt the presence of the Holy Spirit nor experienced any diminution of pain.

Everyone who takes the risk of praying for the sick will encounter this experience many times. When it happens, I hear voices in my head saying, "You're a fraud," "No one will be healed," and "Better give up now." These voices stem from both my insecurities as well as from the enemy. The devil very much wants to prevent anyone from having profound encounters with our heavenly Father. If one of Satan's minions can prevent prayer, he's well on the way to victory, at least for that day.

I gave the young woman my business card and asked her to contact me if she subsequently noticed any significant changes. Sometimes healing is instant, and sometimes it is progressive. Sometimes nothing seems to happen at all. What comforts me is knowing that I can't heal anyone. Anything good that happens during prayer ministry is an expression of God's goodness and mercy. That said, while we can't heal anyone ourselves, it is our responsibility to abide in Jesus Christ so that the power of the Holy Spirit can flow through us. No abiding, no power. While the gifts of the Holy Spirit say little about us, our character speaks volumes. We need self-control to maintain regular prayer and Bible study, courage to keep going when we see little success, and humility to keep the focus on Jesus.

Black Cardigan

The young woman rose from her seat, and we said our good-byes. As she was leaving, I turned around and saw two young female students standing together. I instantly knew one of them was the woman cutting herself. She was indeed wearing a black cardigan over a T-shirt. Even though I knew she was the woman from the movie clip and knew she had been sexually abused, I nonetheless asked her how I could pray for her. However clear, I don't think words of knowledge give us a right just to barge into people's lives. We should always ask the person how we can pray for them. Doing so provides the person with an opportunity to share what's going on in their lives, and that information may be helpful in the time of ministry.

This young woman didn't say anything. She simply rolled up her left sleeve, showing several gruesome red marks where she had cut herself.

I like to ask people their first names when I pray with them. Names are important. Some people have never heard their names used in prayer before. Just hearing their names spoken before God can be a significant experience all by itself, regardless of what does or doesn't happen through the time of ministry prayer. I'm also aware that those who come forward for ministry, especially if they have suffered any form of mental, physical, or sexual abuse, often feel very exposed and vulnerable. Perhaps the abuse has been hidden for years. It's always good practice to ask permission before touching another person in prayer, but it is doubly important to seek consent from anyone you suspect has been abused. The touch might be very well-intentioned, but it might trigger memories of times when physical contact resulted in physical or emotional pain.

I asked her permission to rest my hand on her shoulder, and she agreed. This time the presence of the Holy Spirit was very noticeable. Sensing the presence of the Holy Spirit is not essential for healing to take place. It is, however, encouraging for those ministering and those receiving prayer. In this situation, I could feel the love of the good, good Father for this young woman. I could also sense her self-hatred, her feelings of worthlessness, and her brokenness. I began to pray, slowly and simply.

"Father, thank you that you love Susie. Holy Spirit, would you come now and just wash away her shame and fear. Help her to see herself as you see her. Father, break the power of the lies she has believed about herself. In Jesus' name, I break the power of these lies. Come close, Holy Spirit, and do your work."

Kathie and I waited. We could see Susie's body trembling as the power of the Holy Spirit moved through her. What was most remarkable was that over the next few minutes, her entire countenance changed. As we waited and thanked God for what he was doing, we saw light come into her eyes, and joy radiate from her face. She simply looked like a different person. I don't fully know all that the Lord did in her life that day. After our prayer time, I urged her to speak to one of the chaplains or campus counselors. Susie spoke to a chaplain afterward, and she asked the chaplain to tell her about Jesus. Later that day, she became a brand-spanking-new baby follower of Jesus, which the Bible calls being "born again" (John 3:3).

Four Inches

Kathie and I prayed for several more students until there were only a handful remaining. One of those was the young woman who accompanied her friend wearing the black cardigan. When I first saw this young woman, I assumed she had come to support her friend. However, when her friend left, and this student remained behind, I realized she either wanted prayer for herself or to ask some questions to know how to support her friend.

"How can we pray for you?" I asked.

In response, she put her hands together in the traditional prayer gesture, with each finger touching the finger from the opposite hand. I thought her gesture indicated she just wanted us to pray for her. However, she turned her hands ninety degrees and stretched them out in front of her, much like an Olympic swimmer might do on the starting blocks.

"Look! One arm is four inches shorter than the other. One of my legs is also four inches shorter. I can't walk straight. I was always in trouble with my band director at high school. I couldn't march in a straight line and kept messing up the routines."

We asked her to sit down in almost the same position as the woman in the auto accident with whom we had previously prayed with no visible signs of healing. I knelt in front of the student and asked permission to hold her hands. Kathie similarly requested permission to hold her arm. I closed my eyes for a second and simply prayed, "Grow." Besides holding this woman's hands, instead of her ankles, my prayer was precisely the same. If anything, I had more faith for the healing for the first woman.

The girl began to scream. "Look!" she exclaimed. "Look!"

She was touching her fingers together. Her arms were now clearly of equal length.

"Look," she said again. "I can't do that!" she yelled, touching her extended hands together. "I can't do that! I mean, I can now, but I've never been able to do it. Oh my gosh! Oh my gosh!"

She jumped up. "I have to walk," she said, taking off down the room.

The tears then began to flow.

"I can walk straight," she sobbed. "I can walk straight, and the pain in my hips and back has gone."

She continued to cry tears of joy, and Kathie and I continued to worship the good, good Father.

"Can I give you a hug?" she asked us both.

As soon as she hugged me, the Lord livestreamed another word of knowledge.

"Tell me about your relationship with your dad," I said quietly.

She stiffened. I continued, "I've no idea what your relationship has been like with your dad, but the Lord may want to heal something."

Her tears of joy quickly changed into tears of pain. She confided that her stepdad had abused her.

We asked the Holy Spirit to begin to heal her deep emotional pain. Once again, there was an unmistakable sense of the Holy Spirit's presence. After our time of prayer, she told us she felt completely different. She used words like *lighter*, *free*, and *made new* to describe this change. We thanked the Lord and encouraged her to talk with the university chaplains or counselors to follow up.

Thanksgiving and Reflection

After ministry, I've found it helpful to set aside time for thanksgiving and reflection. I also write down any questions that I have arising from the ministry time. I had both praises and questions as I left Malone University. I praised the good, good Father for his visible work in the young woman who had been cutting her left forearm. The Lord not only worked to initiate healing of some of the deep-seated roots of her self-harm, but the ministry was a step in her journey toward becoming a follower of Jesus. Her encounter with the Holy Spirit convinced her of God's great love for her. We also praised God for the miraculous lengthening of a young woman's arm and leg.

I also had questions. Two young women responded to the same word of knowledge; one was healed instantly, and one experienced no visible improvement. I can think of all kinds of explanations; perhaps I missed something in my prayer for her. Might there have been some demonic strongholds that needed breaking before healing could take place? Maybe her healing would be gradual. I simply didn't know. It remained a mystery to me.

I'm equally puzzled that no one responded to the "neck" word of knowledge. Had I simply made a mistake? Might I have seen the poster in some hospital or doctor's office and dredged up the memory from my subconscious, erroneously believing it was insight from the Lord? I didn't think this was the case, but I know I've made mistakes before, and I'm sure I will again. Perhaps the word was correct, but I didn't communicate clearly. Maybe the person wasn't paying attention or was afraid to come forward for prayer or had to rush away for an important exam. I honestly didn't know.

Weighty Matters

I clearly remember the first time I dared to speak a word of knowledge publicly. In the mid-1980s, I attended a charismatic church in Birmingham, England. During the service, if anyone believed they had a word of knowledge, the practice was to walk to the front of the church, share the word of knowledge with one of the elders, and if he gave permission, to share the message with the congregation. Even though the church had good protocols for handling words of knowledge, in practice, they were few and far between, almost always for emotional or spiritual issues rather than physical healing.

One morning during worship, I kept getting the thought that the Lord wanted to heal a woman's lower back. I tried to dismiss the idea, but it kept popping up again like a spiritual whack-a-mole. The more I wanted to push it from my mind, the more insistent it became. I battled this thought for perhaps ten minutes, hoping someone else would have the same word and initiate the ministry. No one did.

I prayed in my heart, "Lord, would you heal that woman? Thank you."

Surely God would hear my prayer, I reasoned.

The insistence that I had to get up and publicly share my word of knowledge didn't lessen. I went to Plan B.

"Lord, if you want to heal this woman, would you confirm the word through someone else, and I'll assist in the prayer ministry? After all, I've never publicly prayed for healing before."

I thought this a reasonable compromise. I waited, but no one else jumped up.

After what seemed like a long battle, but likely was only a few minutes, I threw in the towel and moved onto Plan C. I got up out of my seat and began a long, lonely walk to the front of the church. I was sure every eye was on me. The front of the church seemed a mile away. I plodded up there, step by step, still hoping that God would give the same word to someone else.

No one else jumped up.

I shared my impression with the pastor. I thought he might intervene; perhaps he'd give the word of knowledge himself. Maybe he'd not allow me to give it; it was my first time, after all.

He let me down badly. He pointed to the microphone and said, "Go up after this worship song is over."

I stood there, waiting, waiting, waiting. It was excruciating. I felt very vulnerable and alone. My mouth was dry. My knees were shaking.

"Ummm," I said, rather hesitatingly, "I think maybe there's someone, a lady I think, with a lower back issue, and I think God may perhaps want to heal it."

I don't think I inspired much faith in anyone. Nonetheless, I continued, "If you think you're that person, I'd like to pray with you."

Nothing happened. No one rushed forward. I could hear the voices whispering in my head, *You're such an idiot. Of course, God wouldn't use you. You have no idea what you're doing.*

The last part was correct. I hadn't a clue.

I waited as long as I dared and was just about to return to my seat when a lady stepped out of her chair and walked forward to meet me.

"I think it may be me. I've been having lower back pains for some time."

I asked if I could place my hand on her back, prayed a bumbling prayer, and both of us walked back to our seats. I was glad it was all over. I was honestly embarrassed. Nothing seemed to have happened. I slipped out of the meeting during the last song. I didn't want to process a postmortem with anyone.

For the next few weeks, I avoided the woman I prayed for like I'd avoid the plague. If I saw her go in one side of the auditorium, I made sure I entered the other side. I was so sure nothing had happened. I simply didn't want to ask her to confirm my suspicion.

After two months, the incident was haunting me. Why had I gone up to give what probably wasn't a word of knowledge? How could I face that woman again? Why was there no power in my prayer? I wanted to move on, forget all about it, stick to what I knew. But I couldn't. I had to find out if anything had happened to bring closure to the incident.

I saw the woman the next week at church. Very sheepishly, I approached her.

"Hi, Margaret," I mumbled, looking down. "I just wondered if anything happened when I prayed for your lower back."

"Gosh, I'd forgotten all about that prayer," she said. "Come to think of it, my back pain has all gone. I've lost a lot of weight and kept it off. That seems to have solved the problem."

I was simultaneously happy and disappointed. I was delighted that the woman's pain was gone. I was disappointed that her healing appeared to have resulted from weight loss rather than through my prayers. I've since learned two things: (1) God heals in many ways and (2) losing weight is hard. I'd count this as a healing today, no contest at all!

Practice, Practice, Practice

I included my thoughts and feelings during the event to encourage you that we all must start somewhere. I had received no instruction in receiving or giving a word of knowledge and, reluctantly, gave my first in front of a large group. That's not ideal. It's far better if we are trained in a small group setting. If you are like me, you'll make mistakes from time to time, and a small group is just the place to practice while you learn to recognize the voice of the Holy Spirit.

The only way any of us can learn to discern genuine words of knowledge is through trial and error. Somewhat naively, I assumed I'd grow naturally in all spiritual gifts from the get-go. It never dawned on me that I'd have to learn how to use and develop spiritual gifts just as I had to learn anything else in life. In short, I had to practice and learn from my successes and failures. Likely, this will be your experience too.

Speak Up

As messy as my first attempt to give a word of knowledge was, I did one thing right: I spoke it out. There have been times when I've been convinced God wants to heal someone with a specific condition. Regardless of how much I pray, if God has given me a word of knowledge, no healing has ever happened until I spoke the word of knowledge aloud. When it comes to words of knowledge, I've never found God has been impressed by my efforts to go incognito. It's as if God is saying, "If you believe me for the healing, believe in me enough to speak it out before it happens." And, so that you know, I still get nervous when I give words of knowledge. It's always a risk. But miracles and healings only happen when we take these risks, so I'm all in, even if I make a fool of myself from time to time.

Eye Eye

There are other reasons why it's essential to speak out words of knowledge. Sometimes people mishear and get healed anyway! In September 2017, Pastor Gerry Coates asked me to preach at Moundford Free Methodist Church in Decatur, Illinois, before hosting a Greenville University alumni luncheon. I preached in both services on the kingdom of God. At the end of the first service, I gave a few words of knowledge to identify conditions I thought the Lord wanted to heal. One of the words of knowledge came in the form of a livestreamed movie clip of an eyelid twitching continually. Subsequently, I've learned the medical term for this condition is blepharospasm. At the time, I didn't know this and just did my best to describe what I saw. I said, "I think there is someone here with a twitching eyelid that the Lord wants to heal."

I then gave several other words of knowledge and began praying with the people who had responded. Just before the second service began, Pastor Gerry came to the front with an older man in tow. Gerry explained that this man had had a stroke the previous year and had lost sight in one eye. He'd visited various eye specialists and had many injections in his eye to try to restore his sight. After seeing no improvement for almost a year, his eye specialist told him that he would never see again out of that eye. He misheard my word of knowledge. He thought I had said "eye" not "eyelid." He believed God anyway and was healed right there in his seat. No one prayed for him at all. Pastor Gerry told me later that a second almost-blind person had regained a significant amount of vision at the same meeting. No one prayed with him either. God healed them just because he can!

Worth the Wait

I used to get concerned if no one responded to my words of knowledge, believing this was a sign that I had somehow misheard or miscommunicated what the Spirit wanted to do. While that may be the case (we all get it wrong from time to time), I'm much less hasty to draw that conclusion today. I have a growing list of people who have contacted me long after I'd given a word of knowledge to tell me the word was for them, but they felt they could not respond for various reasons. For example, one young woman contacted me in May 2020 about a word of knowledge I gave at an evening worship service two years previously. She wrote:

I feel like I should let you know, one time when you spoke you mentioned feeling led to pray for specific people with certain illnesses. One of them was a girl who had been dealing with heavy menses and had gone to different doctors and been prescribed different medications that weren't working. When you said this, I started crying uncontrollably, which is uncharacteristic of me; I don't cry very much. I believe the girl you were referring to was me. I didn't tell anyone at the time and tried very hard to convince myself that it must be someone else, but years later I still feel in my heart that it was me.

I have a rare bleeding disorder that causes me to bleed a lot and not much information is known about it. At the time, I was experiencing a lot of bleeding issues that could not be controlled or explained and I was really worried for my future if the bleeding would continue. I hadn't talked to any of my friends about my bleeding disorder or that I was having problems with it before that service, so I didn't stand to have people pray over me. That much attention makes me very anxious and I didn't want to explain to anyone what was going on. There have been plenty of ups and downs with my bleeding disorder, but thankfully I am doing well now.

> Although it was a bit of a scary experience, it meant a
> lot to me to see how God can work through people and
> show that He loves and cares about me.

Her e-mail was worth waiting for. She remembered the details of this word of knowledge. She knew it was for her but felt she could not respond the day I spoke the word of knowledge. I should add, when I gave this word of knowledge, I invited the person to pray with my wife if this would make it less awkward. It's essential to make it as easy as possible for people to respond to a word of knowledge, particularly if it concerns a potentially sensitive matter.

Upside Down

At other times, the word of knowledge may be correct, but it simply takes the person some time before they contact you. I remember speaking on healing at Light and Life Park in Lakeland, Florida, in January 2017. At the end of the service, I prayed for several people with various ailments. Still, only one gentleman testified to the healing of his shoulder. After our prayer time, he was able to swing his arm over his shoulder without pain. He stayed at the front of the church for quite some time, tears rolling down his cheeks, simply worshiping God. It was beautiful to see. However, I left the meeting discouraged and wrote in my journal that very little happened that morning.

I next visited the church in January 2019. As soon as I walked through the door, Pastor Eldred Kelley grabbed my arm and took me to meet one of the ladies from the congregation.

"I'm so glad I got to see you, President Filby," the woman began. "Do you remember praying for me a couple of years ago?"

I remembered praying for the woman, but I needed her to remind me of what we prayed about. She told me her story:

> When I was a small girl, I watched older girls in my neighborhood hang upside down from tree branches, and I copied them. I loved hanging upside down, with my knees hooked over a branch. The world looks so different that way up! Some of the older girls learned to hang upside down using only their ankles. Of course, I wanted to copy the older girls, and I also learned to hang upside down by my ankles. One day I fell. I don't know what happened, perhaps the branch was wet or something. Anyway, when I fell, I damaged my neck and back, and I have been in pain ever since. That was over sixty years ago. I've had five major surgeries since the accident, but none of them fixed the pain. After you preached, I went forward for prayer. Even when I was walking back to my seat, I felt something was different. President Filby, I want you to know I've been in pain almost all my life. But God healed me the day you prayed for me. I've been pain-free for two years now. It's wonderful. Praise the Lord!

Of course, all too often, we neither see healing nor hear about it afterward. This is discouraging, no matter how experienced we are in livestreaming the Holy Spirit's gifts. The temptation is to stop praying for others so we don't have to deal with the disappointment. However, when we stop giving words of knowledge and praying for people with various illnesses and ailments, we also stop seeing anyone healed. I've found a better option is to ask the Lord to give us more words of knowledge, not fewer, so that we move up the learning curve more quickly.

Over to You: Quietly Does It

For a year, I worked with a remarkable economist in San Diego who had the habit of speaking very softly. To listen to her, everyone had to stop talking and lean in, cutting out as much noise as possible. She spoke very softly but always had important things to say. I often think of her when I'm asking the Lord to give me words of knowledge. I need to become quiet on the inside, stop talking, and listen carefully. Words of knowledge are often so fleeting and soft. They are not identified with a big sign saying, "Word of knowledge; pay attention, buddy." They are often the quietest thoughts that fleetingly pass through your mind. You'll certainly miss them if you are not paying attention.

If I'm preparing for an event where I think the Lord may want to use me to pray for healing, I always find time to prepare. I begin with a time of thanksgiving. I remind myself of who God is and his love for those I'll be meeting. I then simply tell the Holy Spirit that I'm available and ask if there are certain people with whom he wants me to pray. Then I simply wait. I invite you to do the same, whether you are speaking in a church, attending a small group, or only heading off for your weekly shop. If a thought or picture flashes through your mind, just write it down. The word of knowledge may have nothing to do with healing. I've had words of knowledge about people's favorite clothing, conversations they've had, and meaningful places they have visited. All the word of knowledge does is help identify people to whom God wants to minister. Sometimes, I have no idea what I'm meant to pray about until I pray for the person. One time, I had a word of knowledge about a woman's rain boots, and I described them in detail. The woman who owned those boots came forward for prayer. God profoundly ministered to her during our prayer time, although the ministry had nothing to do with her multicolored, polka dot, white rain boots at all! The word of knowledge simply helped the woman respond.

As you are waiting, perhaps you'll feel pain in your body in an area where you didn't previously have a problem. This might be a word of knowledge. Write it down.

It's also possible that during your time of preparation, you might hear nothing at all. That's fine too. We can't force the Holy Spirit to give us words of knowledge; all we can do is be available. During the day, if an unusual thought passes through your mind, write it down.

The only way to find out if your pictures, thoughts, or pains are from the Holy Spirit is to test them out. If you are at a small group, for example, you could say something like this: "I'm trying to learn how the Holy Spirit talks to me, and I need your help. When I was praying about our time together tonight, I had several impressions. I'm just going to speak them out in case one or more of them is really from the Lord. If you resonate with one of these words, would you let us know so we can pray with you?" This humble, low-key approach is much preferable than going in proclaiming: "The Lord told me such and such." You'll find that people, as well as the Lord, give grace to the humble but resist the proud.

Questions for Reflection and Conversation

1. Think back over your life. Can you think of times when the Holy Spirit may have given you a word of knowledge that you dismissed as just one of your thoughts?

2. Why do you think words of knowledge are often so fleeting and soft? What might the Holy Spirit be trying to teach us by communicating with us in this way?

3. Spend some time praying short prayers throughout the day: "Holy Spirit, I am available," or, "Holy Spirit, help me to hear you."

4. In Ephesians 1:17–19, Paul prayed:

> "I keep asking that the God of our Lord Jesus Christ, the glorious Father, may give you the Spirit of wisdom and revelation, so that you may know him better. I pray that the eyes of your heart may be enlightened in order that you may know the hope to which he has called you, the riches of his glorious inheritance in his holy people, and his incomparably great power for us who believe."

Pray these words for yourself and the members of your small group.

THREE

that's bananas

We have different gifts, according to the grace given to each of us. If your gift is prophesying, then prophesy in accordance with your faith.

—Romans 12:6

I had no idea who she was.

I was worshiping among several hundred students at a late-night, student-led worship service, part of Greenville University's New Student Orientation in 2013. I had only recently become Greenville's twelfth president, and this was my first incoming class. Several rows in front of Kathie and me, I saw this young woman raise her hands in worship. There was nothing unusual about that at Greenville University. I didn't think any more about it. Yet, as I worshiped, I noticed her, or more specifically, how she was worshiping.

Going to university is a big deal. It's both exciting and scary. Students look forward to new opportunities but are often concerned about making friends, fitting in, succeeding in class, or getting playing time on their team. All are very understandable anxieties. That's exactly how I felt when I began university, minus the concern about playing on a team. That was never going to happen!

Students navigate these challenges in very different ways. Some students play it cool, trying to identify the in crowd to befriend. Some shyly remain on the outside, hoping to befriend just one or two others in their residence halls. This nervousness was evident in this chapel service too. Many students waited to see how others responded before beginning to worship themselves. I've also seen people like this young woman. She was different. It appeared she didn't care what anyone else thought or did. She had decided to worship with her whole heart and soul, abandoning herself in worship. I couldn't see her face. All I saw was her shoulder-length brown hair, height, and the way she expressed her love for God in her hands and body movements. I thanked God for bringing her to Greenville University.

Just as worship was finishing, the Holy Spirit livestreamed this compelling thought to me: "Pray with her."

I knew it was the Holy Spirit speaking to me. I also knew it might be challenging to do. In just a few minutes, hundreds of students would simultaneously be moving in every direction. I couldn't see her face, so I knew I wouldn't be able to recognize her later. If I lost sight of her head, it would be game over.

I turned to Kathie, pointed out the student, and asked Kathie to help me meet the student after the service.

"Do you see her? I asked Kathie. "Quite petite, the fifth person from the right?"

"The one with the shoulder-length brown hair?"

I nodded. Kathie now had her in her sights.

One of the student leaders prayed and dismissed us all. It was game on! It was like a mega shell game, but instead of trying to follow a small ball hidden under one of three shells, I would have to follow one head moving among hundreds of others, all moving in different directions. Kathie went one way, and I headed another, both of us trying to find a way through groups of students without losing sight of her head.

Kathie reached her a few seconds before I did, and we introduced ourselves. She told us her name was Kaylee.

"Hi, Kaylee," I began. "I saw the way you were worshiping, and I simply wanted to tell you your worship brought joy to my heart. Would you mind if we prayed with you?"

She agreed. We simply began to thank God for her. While we were praying, the Holy Spirit streamed another instruction: "Tell Kaylee, 'The Lord delights in you.'"

I kept praying. "The Lord delights in you," seemed like such a small thing to say. She knew that already.

I had the impression again: "Tell her, 'The Lord delights in you.'"

I obeyed this time.

"Kaylee, I don't know if this will mean anything to you, but I keep hearing the Lord tell me to tell you, 'The Lord delights in you.'"

A great big ear-to-ear smile spread across her face.

"President Filby, that's amazing! I've been unpacking today and just put up a whiteboard in my room. Guess what I wrote on it this afternoon? 'The Lord delights in me.' That's such a confirmation I'm in the right place."

Do you think she was encouraged? Absolutely! God wanted her to know he knew everything about her. He'd even seen what she'd written on her whiteboard earlier that day. As is usually the case, I had no idea why "The Lord delights in you" might be meaningful to her. I was simply the messenger boy for this simple five-word prophecy. That's all that was needed, five words.

It would have been so very easy not to speak those five words. It was apparent that this young woman already knew God loved her. The prophecy was so short and unspectacular. Yet, if I hadn't spoken those five words, both of us would have missed an opportunity to experience God doing something special.

Kaylee told me later, "When you came to pray for me, I was utterly overwhelmed by the power of the Holy Spirit and

God's love for me. I was humbled to be loved so well by the Lord. Who was I that he thought enough of me to not only speak to me, but to speak to me through the president of the university? That night, I called my dad just to boast in the Lord and all that he had done! We both cried, knowing I was exactly where God wanted me."

God counts every hair on our head and, apparently, he knows what we write on our whiteboards too. Isn't he marvelous?

Take My Hand

In summer 1982, I co-led a two-week evangelism team for British Youth for Christ (BYFC) in Stalybridge, Greater Manchester. Each morning, the BYFC team prayed together before hitting the streets, parks, and shopping precinct to tell people about Jesus and invite them to our evening meeting. One morning during our prayer time, I was praying for one of our team members when the words "Take my hand" began flashing through my mind. I knew these words were not my own. I neither had a romantic interest in this woman nor had old Beatles' songs running through my head. I wasn't thinking about holding anyone's hand at all. Nonetheless, the words kept coming into my mind. I remembered reading that when the Lord wants us to bring a prophetic word, he some-times gives us the first few words of the message. We speak out these words, trusting that God will provide us with the rest of the message. Somewhat cautiously, I began, "The Lord says, 'Take my hand.'"

As soon as I said, "Take my hand," more words started to flow. Afterward, the woman was silent. She later told me I had prophesied things over her that only she and God knew. She found the words enormously helpful. I was both encouraged and perplexed. When I prophesied, I didn't feel any rush of emotion. It felt natural and ordinary, like speaking to a friend. Other than the sense that the Holy Spirit inspired these words, they were no different from any other words I said. Nonetheless, the words were significant to this woman, in quite deep and profound ways.

Every time the Lord wanted to use me to prophesy during the next year, the words "Take my hand" started running through my mind. It felt like the Holy Spirit was giving me training wheels to help me to get started. I certainly needed them.

Over the next few months, I gave several prophetic words to individuals, and they were all well received. However, I'd never prophesied in a church service to an entire congregation. When this finally happened, those familiar words "Take my hand" began flashing in my head. My heart started pumping like a race car engine. Rather hesitatingly, I walked to the front of the room to tell the church pastor that I thought I had a prophetic word. When the pastor asked me to give him the gist of the word, all I could tell him was the first three words, "Take my hand." I explained the Holy Spirit never livestreamed the message until I took this first step of faith. I was honestly surprised the pastor allowed me to give the prophetic message. I was shaking like a leaf. No doubt, he realized it had taken all my courage even to ask.

Once again, words came to my mind as soon as I began to speak. I was even more nervous after I'd finished. I was genuinely concerned that someone would stand up and say, "I think you missed that one, Ivan! I don't think that was inspired by the Holy Spirit at all."

Instead, the speaker delayed giving his message, simply saying, "We've heard from the Lord this evening. Let's pause and pray to make sure we don't miss anything God wants to do tonight."

I left the meeting encouraged and energized, a very different experience to my feelings of confusion and defeat after giving my first word of knowledge (discussed in the previous chapter). What made these experiences so different? Simply this: I received immediate encouragement after speaking out the "take my hand" prophetic word, but I received no feedback at all after sharing the word of knowledge and praying for the woman's back. I recognize that was partly my fault—after all, I did slip away from church early. However, had a church leader given me a call later that week to debrief and instruct me, I'm sure I would have found the confidence to speak with the woman I'd prayed with much earlier. In hindsight, I'm thankful that these experiences were so different. They remind me how important it is to encourage those learning to minister in the power of the Holy Spirit.

Every prophetic word I gave in 1982 and early 1983 began precisely in the same way with "Take my hand." Perhaps the Holy Spirit had used other ways to get my attention during that time. If he had, I certainly didn't recognize them. If God wanted me to prophesy, I reasoned, he'd simply give me these three words, and I'd be ready to speak out in faith. I honestly thought I'd hear them for the rest of my life. That didn't happen. Hearing these words stopped just as suddenly as they had started. When these words stopped coming, I was both confused and concerned. Did God no longer want me to prophesy? Had I done something to grieve the Holy Spirit? At the time, I had no answers. Looking back, I can clearly see I was relying too heavily on hearing those words. I relied on the formula of listening for these three words and speaking rather than relying totally on the Holy Spirit. If my prophetic gifting was to grow, God needed me to ditch the training wheels. Like any good dad or mom, he simply took them off one day, gave me a great big shove, and shouted, "Pedal!"

That's Bananas

Nowadays, the Holy Spirit might prompt prophecy through words, a picture, a feeling, a thought, or a knowing. Regardless of how the insight comes, delivering it always involves faith. As the apostle Paul wrote: "We have different gifts, according to the grace given to each of us. If your gift is prophesying, then prophesy in accordance with your faith" (Rom. 12:6).

First, we need faith that the insight is from God. Second, we need faith that the prophetic word will have a positive impact. Finally, we need the confidence to begin speaking when the Lord only gives us the first few words of the prophetic message—even more so when the first words seem crazy!

In 1994 Kathie and I visited Jūrmala, Latvia, to help a fledgling church tell its surrounding community about Jesus. During the daytime, we visited high schools, community centers, and churches to talk about Jesus. We invited everyone we met to come to our evening services.

During one of the evening services, I looked around the congregation to see how many visitors had come. As I turned around, I saw the oddest thing. Several rows behind me sat a young and rather muscular woman. She was not smiling. That was not unusual. During the Soviet era, many people learned not to smile. What was odd was that the Holy Spirit was livestreaming to me a picture of a banana sitting on her head. Now that's the sort of thing that will get your attention. You don't see that kind of thing every day! What on earth was God doing? I couldn't make head nor tail of this livestream. In any case, there was nothing I could do about it right then, as Pastor Bob Perry was about to bring the message. When he'd finished preaching, I picked up my things, looked behind me, and still saw the banana again, right there on that woman's head. This time, I felt the Holy Spirit say to me, "Go tell that woman that 'God sees her like a banana.'"

Far be it from me to tell God he doesn't know what he's doing, but that didn't seem like a winning strategy to me. Once again, I had the same strong impression: "Go tell that woman that 'God sees her like a banana.'"

That's all I had, nothing else. I had to make a choice. Was I going to obey God and do something that seemed insulting and downright stupid, or was I going to walk away? I did what every good husband should do in this type of situation: I asked my wife. If she thought the banana impression was crazy, I'd be off the hook.

Kathie looked at me, raised her eyebrows, and told me to get a translator. I headed over to Jana, one of the Russian-English translators we'd met in the church, and asked for her help. I had heard Jana pray just a couple of days before. She had an incredible passion for Jesus. Even to this day, I've heard few people pray with the intensity of this seventeen-year-old Russian girl. I asked Jana if she would be willing to translate a prophetic message I believed I'd received from the Holy Spirit. She kindly agreed. I thought it only fair to give her a fuller briefing.

"The word doesn't make any sense to me now, but I've been hanging around with the Holy Spirit long enough to know he is up to something; I just don't know what."

I could tell my explanation didn't inspire great confidence in Jana.

Kathie, Jana, and I found a pathway through the chairs to reach the woman just as she gathered her things to leave. The woman looked very puzzled and a little disconcerted, I think, when she realized three people were heading her way.

I began, sounding more confident than I felt.

"Jana, would you tell this lady that I think I have a message from God for her? Would she be willing for me to share it with her?"

I wasn't sure where to look. Should I look at Jana when I spoke to her or to the woman with whom I wanted to communicate? It was all slightly awkward. I decided to look at Jana to make sure she fully understood what I wanted her to translate.

Jana, with great intensity, said something in Russian. I didn't understand a word.

I looked at the woman to see how she'd respond. As soon as I looked at her, she looked at Jana. It was proving difficult to catch her eye. This only added to the discomfort of the situation. But at least she agreed and said, "Dah."

"Jana," I continued, somewhat awkwardly, "please tell her 'The Lord sees you like a banana.'"

Jana's head shot up, and she looked straight at me, wide-eyed. "What?" she questioned. Her intonation led me to believe she was questioning my sanity, as well as my message.

I was embarrassed, and I could feel a blush spreading across my face. I confided to Jana, "I don't understand it either, but tell her, 'The Lord sees you like a banana.'"

I could tell Jana felt discomfited too. I was a foreigner just visiting her town for a couple of weeks. She was a local, about to say something potentially insulting to another local woman, someone she might perhaps meet again in the street. I knew this could all go rather badly for her. Nonetheless, Jana translated the message, a little too loudly for my liking. Heads began turning our way. I couldn't understand what she said, but I thought I caught the word banana somewhere in the sentence.

Thankfully, as Jana was finishing her sentence, the Holy Spirit livestreamed the rest of the message. However, the gap between my sentences was long enough for the woman to look from Jana to me with a very puzzled look on her face. I continued, "Jana, please tell this lady that "The Lord sees her like a banana, and today he's going to peel the hard skin away from her heart.' Would she let me pray with her?"

Again, Jana translated with great intensity.

I had no idea how the woman would react. I wondered if she would gather her things, push past us, and head for the door. But she didn't. She put her things down on the chair next to her and said, "Dah."

I could hear Jana whisper a barely audible sigh of relief.

"Jana, would you ask her if she'd allow me to put my hand on her shoulder when I pray?"

Jana translated again. I didn't understand any words this time. Once again, the woman agreed.

Kathie, Jana, and I placed our hands on the woman's shoulder, and I began to pray: "Lord, thank you for this lady. Thank you for loving her so much. Thank you that you will peel the hard skin from her heart today so she can love you. Amen."

I have no idea if Jana translated my prayer or if she just caught a wave of the Holy Spirit herself. She prayed long, loudly, and as passionately as I've ever heard anyone pray.

As Jana was praying, tears began to run down this woman's cheeks. Her whole countenance changed. She began to smile, and she continued to cry with joy. Then, to my surprise, she reached out, grabbed me, and gave me a big bear hug. She was strong. I was sure she must have represented Russia or Latvia in the shot put. I thought she was going to crush me. When she eventually let go, I knew I had been hugged very well indeed. Defensively, I took a step back. I wasn't going to let that happen again anytime soon.

Proverbs 3:5–6 reminds us to "Trust in the LORD with all your heart and lean not on your own understanding; in all your ways submit to him, and he will make your paths straight." If I'd relied on my understanding, I'd have walked away and sought some professional counseling. I would never have experienced God working in this unique way, and the woman would have left unchanged.

I later learned that this woman had attended several services out of curiosity but seemed very hardened to the gospel of Jesus Christ. Most people had heard nothing about Jesus during the Soviet era, and she was curious about this "Western" idea. To this day, I have no idea how or why the word about a banana impacted her this way. Perhaps her father was a fruit grower; maybe she liked that curved yellow fruit. I have no idea. What I know is this: even when I think the Lord's plans seem bananas, he knows what he's doing.

Coffee, Tea, and Prophecy

It was a beautiful sunny morning in San Diego in October 2013. I was waiting in line at Bobby B's, the coffee shop on Point Loma Nazarene University's campus. I'd just started working as the dean of the Fermanian School of Business, and few people on campus knew me yet. While waiting in line, I suddenly understood the Holy Spirit wanted to use me to give a prophetic word to someone in the coffee shop. There were only two obstacles: I neither knew which of the thirty or so customers I should speak to, nor had I any idea what I should say.

The first step was to find the person God had in mind. I looked at each person in turn and asked the Lord, "Is it him? Is it her?"

I looked from person to person until I knew who it was. I honestly don't even know how to describe how I knew. It was like the faintest click in my spirit. I've never cracked a safe in my life, but from what I've seen on the movies, expert safecrackers can hear the tiniest click when one part of the lock disengages. When I looked at this young woman several people ahead of me in the line, I felt that click in my spirit.

She found a seat while I continued to wait for my turn to order. After ordering, I pulled out a business card and approached her.

"Excuse me. I'm Ivan Filby, the new dean of the Fermanian School of Business. While I was waiting in line, I felt the Lord give me a word for you. Here's my business card. Send me an e-mail if you'd like to find out more."

By then, my coffee was ready, and I was late for a meeting. I had to say goodbye and rush.

I'd now found the person but still hadn't the foggiest idea what I was meant to say to her. I describe it as being pregnant with a prophetic word. I knew the prophetic message was growing inside me; it just wasn't quite ready to be born.

After my meeting, I returned to my office and discovered the student had already e-mailed me. I responded, and we agreed to meet later in the week.

After finalizing a report, I headed for a lunch reception next door at the Center for International Development. I sat down at my assigned table. Guess who sat down next to me? You're right! The student from the coffee shop. After lunch, we lingered for a few moments. I told her I still had no idea what the Lord would have me say, but I'd welcome the opportunity to pray with her. I asked permission to put my hand lightly on her shoulder and simply prayed for her. I can no longer remember what I prayed, but it was obviously significant to her. I could see a tear trickling down her cheek.

"Dr. Filby," she told me, "there's no way you could know this, but the words you used in your prayer are the same words my parents have prayed over me every day of my life. I can't wait to tell my mom and dad. They'll be so encouraged to know God has heard every one of those prayers."

How does that happen? I had no idea I was prophesying while I was praying. In my mind, I was just praying for this student. How did I livestream precisely the same words as her parents prayed over her throughout her life? That can only happen by the inspiration of the Holy Spirit. The prophetic word didn't give her or her parents any new information. It just gave them tremendous encouragement that God had been listening to their prayers all along. Of course, they knew from Scripture that God heard their prayers. It's one thing to know this truth by faith; it's another thing entirely to listen to the prayers repeated back to you word-by-word by a stranger.

In this instance, I had no idea I was prophesying. That's not usually the case. In most cases, we know we have a prophetic word to bring. While it's God's job to watch over his word to see that it comes to pass (see Jeremiah 1:12), it is our responsibility to give prophetic words clearly and accurately. We can do great harm to individuals and churches if we are not careful with our words and don't watch our attitudes. Prophetic words should liberate people and lead people to Jesus; something is seriously wrong if people feel manipulated or controlled by a prophetic word. We must put safeguards in place to protect the person prophesying and the person receiving the message to ensure we don't dishonor the Lord through sloppy delivery or impure motives.

Develop Good Prophetic Practice

If possible, I like to ask myself a series of questions before I bring a prophetic word. Of course, in situations where you don't even realize you are prophesying or only have the first few words, that's impossible.

Question One: What has the Holy Spirit revealed?

The Holy Spirit might communicate by bringing a picture to your mind, using a movie clip–style vision, or by your only having a feeling or a sense of knowing. Often, he will use a combination. Before saying anything, it's essential to gather the facts. What did you see? What did you hear? What did you feel? What do you think you know? At this stage, you likely have no idea what the picture or movie clip means.

You won't know which features of the prophetic picture will
be most meaningful to the recipient. Carefully look at what
you see and think how best to describe it. What's happening
in the foreground? What's happening in the background? Are
there any particularly vivid colors? If you see a movie clip, note
the order in which events unfold. Be careful not to dismiss
anything you see or hear as unimportant. This is not the time
to make sense of the word; it's the time to gather the facts so
you don't forget anything.

Question Two: What does it mean?

We need the Holy Spirit's inspiration just as much to help
us interpret a picture as to receive it. For example, if God
shows you an image of a diamond when you are praying for
an unmarried man or woman, it would be easy to assume an
engagement is somewhere on the horizon. Perhaps that's the
correct interpretation, but maybe it's not. Maybe the woman
had stolen the diamond, and the Lord wants to convict her.
Perhaps he's an artist, and the Lord wants to encourage him to
include new and vibrant colors in his work. Maybe she's sharp-
tongued and cuts people like an industrial diamond. Here's
my rule of thumb: unless the Lord gives you the interpretation, don't interpret it. You're just as likely to misinterpret it as
you are to get it right. I recommend you simply describe what
you've seen, heard, sensed, or think you know, and ask them if
it's meaningful. The recipient will often know, but not always.

If they have no idea what the picture means, just ask them to pray about it and leave it at that. If God is speaking, he will make it clear.

Question Three: Do I need to say anything at all?

Sometimes the Holy Spirit will give insight into a person's circumstances simply to help you effectively intercede for them rather than to share the word with them. I've found this less common, but it does happen from time to time.

Question Four: How can I most accurately communicate the revelation?

I find it helpful to rehearse what I want to say in my mind before talking to the individual. If the message seems convoluted to you, it will likely be more confusing to the recipient. Rehearse it until you can clearly communicate what you saw and heard. You might say, for example, "When I was praying for you, I saw a picture of sunlight shining through a brilliant diamond. At first, the sunlight was so bright the diamond's imperfections were obvious. As the sun continued to shine, however, the imperfections started to vanish. I asked God what this meant and got the impression he wants to encourage you. You're not the person you used to be."

Do you see how I first described what I saw before giving an interpretation? Separating revelation from interpretation provides the recipient with space to accept the word but interpret it differently. We should never force our interpretation on others. Communicate clearly and then let the Lord do his work.

I find it helpful to pay attention to the tone of my delivery. I remember bringing a prophetic word to Cornerstone Christian Church, my home church in Dublin, Ireland, in an overly harsh tone. I had to apologize to the congregation and redeliver the word, this time with the gentleness the Lord intended. We must be careful not to allow any frustrations we have in our own lives or with the person we are speaking with to distort the Lord's tone, which is often very loving and gentle.

Question Five: Do I have pure motives?

Spiritual gifts are intended to help you serve others, not to lord it over them. They are powerful expressions of God's love designed to lead people to Jesus and not point them to you. We should not give prophetic words to get people to like us or think better of us. It's always good practice to have someone else present when you prophesy. They can assist in any ministry but also ensure that everything is aboveboard. If you can record the prophetic word on your cell phone, even better. Kathie and I have a collection of old cassette tapes containing prophetic words spoken over us over the last thirty years. We get them out from time to time and listen to them again. Quite often, words that made no sense to us when they were given now seem crystal clear.

Let me show you how I used this framework in real life.

The Girl in the Shower

Kathie and I attended the New Room Conference in the fall of 2018. One evening, we were delayed arriving at Brentwood Baptist Church, the conference venue, by the slow-moving Nashville traffic. When we finally arrived, the evening service was about to begin. It was a very crowded auditorium, but we finally spotted a couple of open seats in the middle of a row and made our way over to them.

We did not know anyone sitting behind, beside, or in front of us. These were just the first open seats we spotted. We put down our Bibles and notebooks, draped our sweatshirts over the back of our seats, and stood, ready to worship. During the worship, I noticed a woman in her late twenties or early thirties standing in the row just in front of us. As soon as I saw her, the Holy Spirit livestreamed a movie clip vision into my mind. To be honest, the movie clip made me uncomfortable.

Question One: What has the Holy Spirit revealed?

What did I see? I saw a shower curtain hanging over a bath. Through the shower curtain, I could just see the faint silhouette of a young girl bent double in the shower. As she stood under the running water, I saw her gradually straighten up, until she was standing up straight, holding her hands up in the air, obviously worshiping. I had the impression that the girl was being set free from difficult circumstances that negatively impacted how she valued herself. The running water was washing away all her spiritual and emotional chains and setting her free. The livestream's final scene showed the woman standing in front of me at the conference, reaching out and wrapping the shower curtain around the girl, making her feel loved, safe, and secure.

Question Two: What does it mean?

I didn't know. I did not know who was in the shower. All I saw was a faint silhouette of a young girl. I could not guess how the woman at the conference would interpret this livestream, but I was confident she would find it meaningful. I wondered whether the woman worked in children's ministry or for some social service agency caring for children. But I didn't know for sure. The only way I would discover its meaning was to share the livestream with the woman.

Question Three: Do I need to say anything at all?

I had never met the woman at the conference, and I wasn't sure how to interpret the livestream. I concluded I needed to share this insight with the woman in case it was meaningful.

Question Four: How can I most accurately communicate the revelation?

This required some careful thought. How should an almost sixty-year-old guy tell a young woman he saw a picture of a girl in a shower? I didn't want her to yell out "pervert" and slap my face in front of almost three thousand people.

What did I do? First, I tried to describe to myself what I saw. It was potentially a very sensitive subject matter. I suspected the young girl was struggling with some significant personal issues.

During the sermon, I rehearsed in my head what I wanted to say to her:

"Excuse me," I'd begin. "During worship, I had this prophetic picture for you. I don't know what it means. I'm wondering if you'd allow me to share it with you in case it's meaningful?"

I'd then introduce her to my wife, Kathie. I wanted this woman to know I was married and was not some random pervert who'd snuck into the meeting to hit on younger women.

I'd describe the movie clip and ask if it meant anything to her. I'd then offer to pray with her. It was all settled in my mind. As soon as the service ended, I was ready for action.

Ah! The best-laid plans of mice and men. Before the speaker had finished his last point, before the final worship song had ended, and before the traditional end of service blessing was spoken, this woman picked up her things, grabbed her jacket, excused herself, and left the auditorium.

Life is full of surprises! Now, what should I do?

During the service, I'd noticed the woman had spoken with the woman sitting to her left. I had no idea if they were friends, or if they'd only just met. There was only one way to find out. I'd have to ask.

"Excuse me," I asked. "Do you happen to know the lady sitting next to you, the one that left before the end of the meeting?"

She did. They'd come to the conference together. I introduced myself.

"Hi, I'm Ivan Filby. I serve as president of Greenville University. During the worship time, I kept seeing a prophetic picture for your friend. I wanted to share it with her in case it was important. Do you know if she'll be coming back tonight? If so, I'd be happy to wait."

"No, she had something else important to do tonight and had to leave a little early."

Time for Plan B.

"If I describe it to you, would you mind passing it on to your friend in case it is meaningful? It's a little strange, but I get the impression it's somehow important."

Her friend agreed. I described the livestream and handed her my business card. I also gave her my cell phone number in case her friend had any questions.

Question Five: Do I have pure motives?

I'd never seen this woman before. I'd likely never see her again. I had nothing to gain by giving this word. I felt my motives were pure.

The following day my cell phone dinged at 6:45 p.m. It was a text message:

> Hey there, Ivan. My name is Regina. I'm the person you had the vision for last night. My friend shared your word with me, and "wow" is all I can say! My niece is in foster care right now and has been having a tough time. Anyhow, I was praying for her last night and asking God for a vision for her. I've been praying about whether to try and seek custody of her.
>
> Anyhow, I hope the conference was a blessing to you. I would love to talk and hear the word God gave you if you are willing. Thank you for taking the step of faith and sharing what I know must have felt crazy. I can't tell you what a gift it was to me when my friend shared this morning.

I called Regina and we spoke for about twenty minutes. Here's how she interpreted the livestream: She had a young niece struggling with various issues. Regina had been praying about whether she should seek custody of her niece to help her navigate the challenges she was facing. That very day, Regina had asked God to give her a clear sign as to whether she should seek custody. She interpreted the scene where she hugged the girl through the shower curtain as the confirmation she needed.

Here's the amazing thing: Kathie and I *happened* to sit in random seats behind her. The Lord *happened* to livestream a movie clip to me that made no sense to me but meant the world to Regina. A lot seems to just *happen* when we take the risk of livestreaming the love and power of the Holy Spirit. I honestly don't know how God orchestrates events like this. It's beyond me. However, we do know this: he loves us more than we deserve, more than we expect, and beyond all we can ever imagine. That's good news.

Over to You: Words of Encouragement

From time to time I'm asked to speak at a pastors' retreat. When this happens, I always ask for a list of attendees before the event. Once I have the list, I begin to pray slowly over every name in case the Holy Spirit has a word of encouragement for any of the leaders. In 2019, Kathie and I were invited to speak at a pastors' retreat for the Wabash Conference of the Free Methodist Church in the USA. Once I'd received the list of participants, I prayed daily for every pastor before the conference began, but the Lord only gave me one word of encouragement for one pastor. I wrote it down and took it to the conference. During one of the conference ministry sessions, I asked the conference superintendent to point out this pastor to me. He pointed to the one African pastor in the room. I approached him, told him I believed the Holy Spirit had given me a word of encouragement for him, and asked permission to share it with him. He readily agreed. I shared the word with him and showed him where I had written it down on my attendance list. He wept. He told me he had been in the United States for nine years and no one had ever brought him a personal word from the Lord in all that time. He was so encouraged.

The Lord can use you to encourage others just as easily as he uses me. Livestreaming the Holy Spirit's gifts, remember, is not a sign of maturity, but a sign of availability. A little training can help too. Our Western mindset often results in our reinterpreting spiritual phenomena in natural ways. For example, during our prayer times, I think most of us have unexpectedly thought about a childhood friend, a relative we have not seen for ages, or a work colleague. I used to regard these thoughts as distractions, the result of a tired or sloppy mind. Now that I'm more familiar with some of the ways the Holy Spirit leads us, I'm convinced that many of these "distractions" are actually invitations from the Holy Spirit to pray for these people. Nowadays, instead of pushing these thoughts aside, I simply say, "Holy Spirit, how can I encourage Sylvia, Alan, Jonathan, or Marta?" Sometimes, the Holy Spirit livestreams some insights there and then. Often, as I pray for these people during the day, other thoughts pop into my mind. I've lost count of the times I've been thanked for the timeliness of my encouraging words or the relevance of the Scriptures I've shared.

Perhaps during your time of prayer, a face or name might pop into your head. This may be the Holy Spirit indicating people he'd like you to pray for or encourage. If you suddenly start thinking about Great Aunt Maud when you've not thought about her for ages, it may be the Holy Spirit inviting you to pray for her in a more focused way. Even if it's not, the worst thing that can happen is that you pray for her and send her an encouraging note. As worst things go, that's a pretty good one!

In addition to paying attention to the faces and names that pop into your head during times of prayer, I'd encourage you to use your prayer list differently. Instead of merely praying for any known prayer requests, ask the Holy Spirit to give you a scripture or a word of encouragement for one or more of the people you are praying for regularly. When the Holy Spirit gives you something to communicate, give them a call or send them a note. Don't dismiss it if it's only five words. It might be the five words the person really needs to hear.

Questions for Reflection and Conversation

1. Can you think of times when people's faces, names, or situations popped into your mind during your times of prayer? What was it like? What did you do?

2. Write down the names of family members and friends on a piece of paper. Pray over each name slowly each day and ask the Lord to give you a word of encouragement.

3. Find some alone time and ask the Lord to give you a word of encouragement for yourself. A thought or scripture might come to mind. Write a letter to yourself, putting this thought or scripture into words, and then use it to form a prayer for yourself.

4. If you haven't already done this, start a journal and record all the times God gives you an encouraging word for yourself or someone else. Write down what you saw or heard and explain what happened when you told the person.

FOUR

shirt and tie

He sent out his word and healed them.

—Psalm 107:20

"Polyps."

I was preparing to speak at Greenville Free Methodist Church in 2017 when the Holy Spirit livestreamed some words of knowledge to me. I wrote them all down, but one puzzled me: *polyps*. I had no idea what a polyp was, and I had to look up its definition online:

A solitary or colonial sedentary form of coelenterate such as a sea anemone, typically having a columnar body with a mouth uppermost surrounded by a ring of tentacles.

I didn't think it was that definition. I hadn't seen any of those swimming around church recently, and if I had, I'd be out of the church like a shot. I looked to see if there were any other definitions:

A small growth, usually benign and with a stalk, protruding from a mucous membrane.

That sounded more like it. A small benign growth. As soon as I read this definition, I got the impression that there were polyps in a woman's uterus.

I preached at the Greenville church the next morning and gave the words of knowledge in both services. During one ministry time, Kathie called me over. She was praying with a Greenville University student. Kathie asked the student to explain her condition. She told me, "I've recently been diagnosed with polyps on my vocal cords. When I heard you say polyps, I immediately thought you might mean me. One day, when I was a kid, I was playing with friends. I was screaming and shouting so loudly that I damaged my vocal cord. That's a big problem now because I'm a singer. When I sing my scales, I can no longer reach the top notes. Would you pray for me, please?"

I asked her to place her hand over her throat and asked permission to put my hand gently over hers. I then commanded the polyps to go. We had many people to pray with that morning, so we didn't have the opportunity for an extended time of prayer. I simply asked her to let me know if she noticed any improvement over the coming days and weeks.

The following Wednesday, I was heading to the Greenville University chapel when I suddenly heard a student call out, "President Filby! President Filby!"

I turned around to see who was calling and saw this student running toward me.

"Guess what?" she asked.

"What?"

"I went to the music practice room this morning. I was practicing my scales, and I suddenly realized I could sing right up to the high notes for the first time in forever. Thank you for praying with me. Please thank Mrs. Filby too."

I promised I would.

I was excited that God had healed the person with polyps and simply assumed I'd missed the mark when I had the impression that the polyps were in a woman's uterus.

A couple of months later, Kathie received a text from a good friend of ours, Megan. Megan explained that when she heard the word of knowledge in church about the polyps, she sent the following text to one of her friends who suffered from polyps in her uterus.

"President Filby is about to pray for your healing."

I knew nothing about this text. When Megan's friend had her next monthly cycle, she discovered she was completely healed. She was not a member of the Greenville church, and no one prayed with her that morning. All she received was a text from Megan, and God healed her. How does that happen? God certainly moves in mysterious ways.

The Most Important Advice

The most important advice I can give to help you mature in your use of spiritual gifts is to learn to love Scripture. I say learn to love because that's what most of us must do: learn. Few of us have a natural love for Scripture. It's a collection of books written across several centuries by many authors in several languages and very different cultural contexts. These factors alone make it challenging to read well.

Nevertheless, we must learn. God has breathed through this book in unique ways, making it a book like no other. If you are serious about getting to know God well, you'll need this book. You can read Scripture in a variety of ways. You could read huge chunks of Scripture over a few days to understand God's big story and where you fit in. Other times, you might study a theme, such as worship, love, or healing. Nowadays, there's plenty of great resources available free on the Internet to help with this type of study. You could memorize Scripture, meditate on verses, sing Scriptures, read Scripture aloud, or use Scripture to frame your prayers.

Knowing Scripture well, of course, is also essential for weighing prophetic words. Even though God sometimes does unique and surprising things, he never does anything inconsistent with who he has revealed himself to be in Scripture. Furthermore, God will bring Scripture to your mind when you are livestreaming, so the more Scripture you know, the more Scripture the Spirit can bring to your mind during ministry.

If you haven't made reading Scripture a priority, I encourage you not to get all guilt-ridden and immediately commit to reading the Bible for hours each day. That might work for one percent of people, but most will get discouraged, bored, and give up pretty quickly. When I wanted to run a 5K race, I didn't just put my name down on the runners' list and head for the starting line. I used one of the Couch to 5K apps to help me build up my stamina. In Week One, I ran for one minute and then walked for several minutes before running again. In Week Two, I extended my runs to ninety seconds and reduced my in-between walking periods to two minutes. In Week Three, I alternated between running for two minutes and walking for ninety seconds. Each week, I stretched a little further until I was ready for my first 5K.

Interestingly, after a few weeks, I accidentally repeated Week One. The first time I worked through Week One, I was breathless by the end. The second time, it didn't challenge me at all. I'd built up some stamina.

If you haven't read much Scripture, you'll need to build up stamina in the same way as I had to build up endurance to run a 5K. Start small. Perhaps read a psalm one day and a section from one of the Gospels the next. Jot down what you learn and make a note of any questions you have. If any verse strikes you as particularly interesting or relevant, write that down, too, and perhaps use those words to frame your prayers that day.

When we make reading Scripture a priority, not to become know-it-alls, but to learn to love God well and serve others, it's like we are putting down a great big welcome mat for the Holy Spirit, letting him know we're ready for adventure.

If learning to love Scripture puts down a welcome mat, faith puts down the red carpet! I'm sure you are familiar with movie stars walking down the red carpet to attend movie premiers in Hollywood, New York, Cannes, or London. The film production companies roll out the red carpet to honor the movie stars. In just the same way, we honor God when we exercise faith. Faith is his red carpet, and that always draws him close.

Faith

When it comes to healing, faith is always essential; someone must have it, but it doesn't necessarily need to be the sick person. It's particularly unhelpful to tell people they remain sick because of their lack of faith. It's often much harder for the person struggling with ongoing illness to believe for their healing than for others to have faith for them.

You perhaps remember the story from Luke 5:17–39 when some guys tried to bring a sick friend to Jesus for healing. Jesus was debating with some religious busybodies, and a vast crowd came to watch, hoping for a religious rumble. The sick man's friends tried every which way to carry their friend to Jesus, but the crowd was chockablock; they could find no way through. So, what did they do? They lowered their friend down through the roof and rested him on the floor right next to Jesus. Jesus did what he's very good at doing; he made their friend well again. Luke 5:20 says: "When Jesus saw their faith . . ." Isn't that amazing? Jesus didn't mention the sick person's faith at all; he praised the faith of his friends.

The Ugly Leg Brace

One Sunday morning at Cornerstone Christian Church in Dublin, Geraldine asked me to pray for her grandson. I looked down and saw he had an ugly metal leg brace supporting one of his legs. I had no faith for his healing. However, Geraldine was convinced that Jesus would heal her grandson if I prayed for the boy. I prayed for her grandson because I loved Geraldine. She was a mother to many of us in the church. It was Geraldine that had the faith for healing, not me. Whereas I focused on the boy's condition, Geraldine concentrated on Jesus.

Hebrews 11 describes faith as an assurance or evidence of things not seen. Faith is like the title deed on a piece of property. If someone transfers the title document to you, you not only have a legal document in your hand; you also have full rights to the property. Faith is like that; you are sure Jesus will do what he said he would do. I generally know when I have faith and when I don't. I knew I had no faith for Geraldine's grandson's healing. But Geraldine did, and so I prayed. That night, Geraldine's grandson started to complain that his leg brace felt too tight. His parents adjusted it. The next day, he said it was hurting him again. When his parents took off the brace again to fix it, the boy walked away, unaided. He was healed. His parents never put that brace back on.

Here's the good news. We don't need a lot of faith to see God move. Jesus describes the amount of faith you need in terms of a mustard seed; the smallest seed Jesus' listeners would have known. Jesus healed people who had little faith as well as those who had plenty. In Mark 9:17–29, we read the account of Jesus coming down from a mountain with Peter, James, and John. When they got to the foot of the hill, a desperate father ran to meet Jesus. The father explained to Jesus that he'd brought his son to the other nine disciples, but they could not heal him. The father knelt at the feet of Jesus and begged, "If you can do anything, take pity on us and help us."

The dad didn't have much faith. Perhaps understandably so. Jesus' A-team disciples failed to heal the boy. The dad wasn't sure Jesus could heal him either. Jesus picked up on the "if you can" comment and said, "Everything is possible for one who believes."

The dad prayed a great prayer: "I do believe; help me overcome my unbelief." It wasn't great faith, but it was enough for Jesus to heal the boy.

I mentioned earlier that it's vital that we know Scripture. This passage is an excellent example of why knowing Scripture is so important. There are so many insights just in this one passage. Let's put ourselves in this story. Imagine it was you or me who begged the nine disciples for healing. When the boy didn't improve, I bet we'd conclude it just couldn't be God's will to heal him. That's a reasonable conclusion, right? After all, we'd asked Jesus' handpicked special forces to pray for healing. They'd prayed, but nothing happened. There's just one problem with concluding it couldn't be God's will to heal the boy: it's the wrong conclusion. As we see in this story, Jesus heals the boy. Jesus reveals God's will by healing him.

If we pray for someone who doesn't get healed—and there will be many such people—we must not rush to conclude that it's not God's will. It might merely be that we haven't yet learned to pray effectively for people with their condition. This story exemplifies this. When the disciples later questioned Jesus about why they couldn't drive the evil spirit out, Jesus explained that it is only possible to drive out this particular spirit through prayer and fasting. We must be careful concluding something is not God's will just because we are not successful in our ministry. Our responsibility is to keep praying, keep asking others for wisdom, and keep learning. We should never give up.

If there was no improvement in our condition after a visit to the doctor, we'd never conclude that it must not be God's will to heal us. We'd pick up the telephone and make another appointment. Sadly, we give up on prayer all too readily. If we've been prayed for once or twice for healing and don't see any improvement, we give up. By giving up, we might just miss our miracle.

Faith Extenders

God sometimes gives us prophetic pictures to help us to grow in our faith. I call these faith extenders. I'm sure God used them with Abraham. It's hard for us in the Western world to imagine what it's like to look at the night sky without light pollution. When my family moved from Dublin, Ireland, to rural Illinois, we soon noticed how many more stars we could see in the night sky. On cold winter nights, we'd all get into the hot tub, turn out the lights, and look up at the myriad of stars we could see. We even could follow the blinking-light flight paths of aircraft passing way overhead.

Even in this beautiful, rural setting, it was never completely dark. However, for Abraham, other than a fire or ancient oil lamp, all he could see at night was an astonishing number of stars. Millions and millions of them. Breathtaking!

When Abraham looked down, he saw dust. Plenty of it. His feet would get covered with dust. Likely it would blow into his beard and his hair. Most probably, it would work its way under his clothing. He simply could not escape the dust. It was a regular part of Abraham's life.

Similarly, Abraham would have seen plenty of sand as he traveled down the west bank of the Mediterranean Sea during his journey from southern Mesopotamia to the promised land. Abraham was familiar with stars, dust, and sand, and the Lord God used these as focal points to extend Abraham's faith to help him believe God's promises.

In Genesis 13:16, God said to Abraham, "I will make your offspring like the dust of the earth, so that if anyone could count the dust, then your offspring could be counted." A pretty fantastic promise for an older man married to a woman who was well past childbearing years. A little later, when he had one son, Ishmael, God repeated his promise to Abraham, this time telling him to look up:

> The word of the LORD came to him: "This man [Ishmael] will not be your heir, but a son who is your own flesh and blood will be your heir." He took him

outside and said, "Look up at the sky and count the stars—if indeed, you can count them." Then he said to him, "So shall your offspring be." (Gen. 15:4–5)

God reminded Abraham once again of his promise in Genesis 22:16–18. God had just seen Abraham trust God entirely, not even putting his son's life ahead of his obedience to God.

God said to Abraham,

"I swear by myself . . . that because you have done this and have not withheld your son, your only son, I will surely bless you and make your descendants as numerous as the stars in the sky and as the sand on the seashore. Your descendants will take possession of the cities of their enemies, and through your offspring, all nations on earth will be blessed, because you have obeyed me."

God graciously kept reminding Abraham of his promise, even when Abraham saw little evidence that the promise was being fulfilled. Abraham was childless when God first gave the dust promise. He had but one child, Ishmael, when God first told him to look up to the stars. He had two sons, Isaac and Ishmael, when God told him to look up at the stars and down at the sand. Two sons, not exactly a multitude.

Nonetheless, "Abram believed the LORD, and he credited it to him as righteousness" (Gen. 15:6). God used the everyday dust, stars, and sand, ordinary parts of Abraham's existence, to remind Abraham continually of God's promise to Abraham, that he would make him the father of a multitude.

Faith extenders are not just something for ancient times; God still uses them today.

Shirt and Tie

I met Michelle in her junior year of college. She had a deep love for God and was very serious about her faith. On the few occasions we spoke about relationships, she despaired the quality of men who had asked her out on a date. "Those guys are just okay," she told me, "but I simply can't look up to any of them. They're more interested in their PlayStations than in Jesus."

Toward the end of her time at college, she came to my office to talk about life after college, grad school applications, and work opportunities. During the conversation, she asked if I thought she'd ever get married. I never answer those questions unless God gives me some specific revelation. A week or so later, I clearly remember the Holy Spirit livestreaming some instructions for her. When I next saw her, I invited her for coffee.

"This is going to sound crazy," I told her, "but this is what I hear from the Spirit. I'd like you to buy a shirt and a tie you imagine your future husband will wear and hang them in your closet. Think about the size of the shirt. Do you imagine him tall, or broad-shouldered, or slim? Choose the shirt you imagine he might wear. Then, every day you see the shirt and tie hanging in your closet, thank God for this man. God will bring him to you."

A couple of years later, I was shopping with Kathie in a local Walmart when we suddenly heard this loud voice calling out.

"Dr. Filby! Dr. Filby!"

A woman ran down the aisle to meet us.

"Dr. Filby, remember me? I'm Michelle! You prayed for me and told me to buy a shirt and tie for my future husband and hang them in my closet."

"Oh! Hi, Michelle. Of course, I remember you," I said. "How are you?"

She held out her left hand to show us her engagement ring and wedding band. "I'm married," she said with a big smile. "And," she said, pausing for a rather long time, "the shirt fits!"

Did buying the shirt and tie somehow magic up a husband? Not at all. However, I do believe Michelle's response to the prophetic word was significant. Michelle certainly thought so.

A Good Mentor

A good mentor can also help us to develop our faith. My first mentor, Geoff Shipman, the bivocational pastor of Beeston Christian Fellowship just outside Nottingham, England, reminded me repeatedly of prayer's importance to faith development. Geoff was wise, very in tune with the Holy Spirit, but with both feet firmly planted on the ground. There was nothing flaky about Geoff. He was an unlikely prophet: a painter and decorator by trade, who spoke and prophesied with a stutter, but who ministered with incredible prophetic insight and accuracy. Geoff told me that he saw great potential in me but noticed I struggled to use spiritual gifts well.

One of the first areas of weakness he pointed out was my tendency to speak prophetic words prematurely. When I received a prophetic word, I'd want to give it right away. I'd never considered any alternative to this practice. He coached me that when I felt the Holy Spirit had given me prophetic insight for someone, if possible, I should intercede for the person before delivering the message. He kept reminding me that prophetic words should encourage, comfort, advise, or guide, and that intercession increases the word's effectiveness. Using an analogy from Nottingham's most famous son, Robin Hood, Geoff likened spiritual gifts to an arrow in a pull-string bow. If you only pull back the bowstring an inch, the arrow doesn't fly very far. However, if you have the strength to pull the bowstring back to its full extent, the arrow shoots out with power. He explained that intercession helps us pull back our prophetic bowstring, giving the prophetic insights more spiritual power to do their work.

I had the privilege of traveling with Geoff to several churches, often churches with significant difficulties, and the Lord would reveal to him the roots of the issue. One time, I even went with him to a strip mall. All the shop units in the strip mall were profitable, except one. No matter what business was in this particular unit, it always failed. The strip mall owner knew Geoff and asked him to pray in the shop unit and around the strip mall. Geoff invited me to be part of a small team he took with him. During our prayer time, one of the team discerned a spiritual cause for the repeated failures of the units. Geoff prayed and broke the grip of evil. The next shop to move in was profitable.

You Can Do It

A good mentor can discern when to push us beyond our comfort zone. I've found Pastor David Yip, from Joyful Praise Assembly in Hong Kong, particularly good at this. In 2019, he invited me to speak in his church in Kowloon. I suggested I would talk about prayer and the work of the Holy Spirit. David responded, "No, I think we'll have a miracle service." I explained to David that a miracle service was well beyond my level of anointing. He laughed and said, "Too late, we've already advertised the meeting throughout Hong Kong." I was left with no alternative other than to preach and pray.

David translated my message, my words of knowledge, and assisted me during my ministry time. Throughout the ministry time, I kept inviting Pastor David to step in and take over leading. The miracle service was way outside of my comfort zone, but he refused to lead. Every time I'd go to him and ask him to lead, he'd push me back out in front and tell me, "You can do this." He wanted me to learn to stretch in my ministry.

Spiritual Slipstreaming

In many ways, I was able to "slipstream" in David's anointing. Racecar drivers slipstream all the time during their races. A driver planning to overtake the car in front will drive up behind it as close as possible to get into the car's slipstream. The leading racecar creates an area of low pressure behind it that can pull the trailing car along. When the trailing car gets into the slipstream, it can drive as fast as the leading car using less throttle. Just at the right time, perhaps on a bend or a long straight, the trailing driver can apply full throttle to overtake the leading car. Spiritual slipstreaming occurs when we are pulled along by another's anointing, enabling us to do things we'd never have attempted before.

King Saul was a great slipstreamer. He was not a prophet, yet when he met a group of prophets in Gibeah, the Holy Spirit came on him with such power that he also prophesied. He slipstreamed their anointing to the extent that people asked whether Saul "was now one of the prophets" (1 Sam. 10:10–11). The wonderful truth about slipstreaming is that even though we are slipstreaming behind someone else's anointing, it gives us a taste of what is possible. If we can do it once, perhaps we can do it again.

Despite feeling way out of my depth, it turned out to be a service full of miracles, with many people testifying to their healing. One healing was particularly memorable. I'd given a word of knowledge that I believed the Lord wanted to heal a woman with pain in her right hip. Immediately, a woman hobbled up to the front. I asked Pastor David to speak to her in Cantonese to ask her what level of pain she was experiencing on a scale of one to ten. She rated her level of pain as a ten. I prayed a short prayer and asked David to ask her whether the level of pain had decreased. She confirmed it had fallen to an eight. I prayed again. She told us her pain had gone down to a five. I prayed again and asked David to ask if her pain level had decreased any further. He spoke to her in Cantonese, but she didn't respond. I assumed she hadn't heard David's question and asked him to repeat it. He began to laugh. "Ivan, look at her. The Holy Spirit is resting on her so powerfully that she just can't speak! She can't answer your question even if she wanted to." We continued to pray. Eventually, she was able to speak again and told us her pain had gone entirely. I'd never seen the power of God resting so forcefully on anyone that they could not talk.

Shameless Audacity

I learned so much from mentors, not least how to pray boldly and fervently, or as Jesus put it, with shameless audacity. When the disciples asked Jesus to teach them to pray, he taught them

far more than the Lord's Prayer. In the Luke 11 account, Jesus
teaches his disciples:

> "Suppose you have a friend, and you go to him at
> midnight and say, 'Friend, lend me three loaves of
> bread; a friend of mine on a journey has come to me,
> and I have no food to offer him.' And suppose the one
> inside answers, 'Don't bother me. The door is already
> locked, and my children and I are in bed. I can't get up
> and give you anything.' I tell you, even though he will
> not get up and give you the bread because of friendship,
> yet because of your shameless audacity he will surely get
> up and give you as much as you need.
>
> "So I say to you: Ask and it will be given to you;
> seek and you will find; knock and the door will be
> opened to you. For everyone who asks receives; the one
> who seeks finds; and to the one who knocks, the door
> will be opened.
>
> Which of you fathers, if your son asks for a fish,
> will give him a snake instead? Or if he asks for an egg,
> will give him a scorpion? If you then, though you are
> evil, know how to give good gifts to your children, how
> much more will your Father in heaven give the Holy
> Spirit to those who ask him!" (vv. 5–13)

Jesus teaches his disciples that it is this type of prayer that
God answers, whether we are asking for bread for a friend,

healing, or the gifts of the Holy Spirit. Jesus might just as easily have said, "how much more will your Father in heaven give the Holy Spirit to those who ask him with shameless audacity!"

Why Doesn't the Lord Heal Me?

Kathie and I were leading a series of revival meetings for ten to twelve churches on the Illinois-Indiana border with Doug and Margie Newton in Robinson, Illinois, in 2016. I spoke on Thursday and Friday evenings. Doug and Kathie both spoke on Saturday morning, and I wrapped things up on Saturday night. Our theme for the meetings was understanding the kingdom of God. After preaching Thursday night, we had the opportunity to pray with several people. One woman came forward at every opportunity to request healing prayer for significant back pain. She asked us to pray for healing on Thursday and Friday nights. Nothing happened. We prayed for her again early on Saturday morning, during the break between morning sessions, and again before lunch. She experienced no improvement at all. As she headed out for lunch, she asked me, "Why doesn't the Lord heal me?"

That wasn't a theoretical question; it was a question asked in great pain. I was honest and upfront in my response and simply said, "I'm so sorry, I just don't know." As Kathie and I headed off to lunch, I felt the Holy Spirit tell me I needed to be bolder and more forceful in my prayers and not accept no for an answer. I preached again that evening. When I finished teaching, Kathie and I headed over to the woman and asked to pray again.

When I pray with people experiencing physical pain, I often ask them to rate their pain level on a ten-point scale, with ten being excruciating. I ask this question for two reasons. First, it gives us a starting point for prayer. Sometimes healing is instantaneous, but at other times it is gradual. When a person notices the level of pain going down, she or he knows something is happening. It is very encouraging. I also ask people the question to let them know I'm expecting something to happen, which encourages their faith. This woman rated her pain at level ten. We prayed once more; her pain did not lessen. We prayed again. Once more, we saw no improvement. I was very frustrated. I felt I had faith for her healing, and I couldn't understand why she was not improving.

I prayed again. When I asked the woman to rate her pain, she paused, thought about it, and told us it had gone down to an eight. This was very exciting. We prayed yet again, and this time she said her pain went down to a six. We prayed again. She told us her pain lessened again to a four. We prayed once more, and this time she told us she was completely pain-free. In all, Kathie and I prayed ten times for healing, and it wasn't until the tenth time that she was healed completely.

Endorphins

It's worth noting that sometimes people experience a reduction in pain, not because healing is taking place, but because the prayer time has temporarily increased the person's production of endorphins. Endorphins are a group of hormones secreted in the brain and nervous system that, among other things, reduce our experience of pain. When the secretion of endorphins slows down, pain often comes back. Knowing this, I like to check back with the people I've prayed with before talking publicly about their healing. I don't want to celebrate if healing hasn't happened.

Did You Say?

I've noticed that the more we press in with shameless audacity, the more things God does without us asking. Several times I've prayed for one person, and another was spontaneously healed. For example, at a church service in Decatur, Illinois, Kathie prayed for a high school girl who had responded to a word of knowledge I had given about neck and back pain. The girl told Kathie that she had been playing in a swimming pool when a friend jumped on top of her, injuring both her neck and back. Kathie laid one hand on this girl's shoulder and her other on the girl's friend, who was standing beside her. Kathie began to pray for the healing of the girl's neck and back when suddenly her friend started to scream. "Look!" she yelled, "I've stopped shaking!" She had suffered from tremors all her life. God healed her, even though Kathie wasn't praying for her. When the girl with the injured neck saw her friend's healing, her level of faith soared, and she was healed too.

Occasionally, God heals spontaneously in unique ways. In 2015, I was standing in a crowded exhibition hall at the Free Methodist General Conference in Orlando, Florida, representing Greenville University, when I heard someone shout out, "Excuse me!" I didn't take much notice. The exhibition hall was full of hundreds of noisy people talking, catching up, drinking coffee, sharing stories, laughing together, or looking at one of the many exhibitor booths from church ministries and universities. I heard the voice again. "Excuse me. Are you Dr. Filby?"

This time I stopped walking, turned around, and saw this petite older lady walking toward me.

"You are Dr. Filby, aren't you? I thought I recognized you from the Free Methodist Prayer Summit."

The woman introduced herself and told me she was from New York.

"I have a question for you," she stated, quite forcefully. My heart sank like a lead balloon. A university president's work is never easy, and on just about any issue, I suspected I upset as many people as I pleased. I steeled myself for her question.

"When you spoke at the National Prayer Summit, did you say, 'The healing in your foot is starting now?'"

I hadn't expected that question. It took me a few seconds to respond. I thought back over my four sessions. My message was identical in each session, although each ministry time was different. I remembered that during one of the sessions, I had mentioned an incident in which I had prayed for a young woman's foot the day before she was scheduled to have her foot amputated. However, I didn't say, "The healing in your foot is starting now." I confirmed this to the woman.

"Why do you ask?"

"Why do I ask?" she replied. "Well, you see, I'd hardly been able to walk for the last year or two. I had terrible pain in my foot, and it was challenging for me to get about. Anyhow, during your session, I clearly heard someone say, 'The healing in your foot is starting now.' As soon as I heard those words, I felt heat shoot down my leg and through my foot, and the pain went away. It was amazing. Look at how I can walk."

Walk, she did! She took about ten steps in one direction, turned, and walked twenty steps in the other direction before returning to stand in front of me.

"The thing is," she continued, "ever since it happened, I've wondered if it was your voice or God's voice that I heard. It must have been God's," she concluded.

"It must have been," I agreed. "I definitely didn't say it. But," I continued with a wry smile, "if you weren't sure if it was God or me, do you think that means God has an English accent?"

Over to You: Keep it Short

It has taken me many years and lots of failures before I saw any success in healing prayer. This is not uncommon. I remember reading that John Wimber, the founder of the Vineyard Church movement, prayed for hundreds of people to be healed over nine months before anyone was healed. One of the reasons I saw little healing at first was that I didn't pray scripturally. I'd pray, "O, God, please take so-and-so's pain away if it is your will. Amen." Interestingly, Jesus never asked the Father to heal a person; he commanded the condition to be healed. He also never doubted it was God's will to heal. I used to pray long drawn-out prayers. I never asked questions to see if anything was happening, and I never had any way to measure if there was any improvement.

I'm told that when you learn to ski, the hardest part is learning to lean forward when instinctively you want to lean back. Praying for healing is a little like that; you must lean in. Begin by asking the person their name and use their name in your prayer. Ask the person their level of pain and range of movement. These are excellent ways to assess if any healing has taken place. It is very encouraging when a person experiences an increase in their range of motion or a reduction in pain.

Then pray short, simple prayers, commanding the condition to be healed and ask the person if anything has changed. Nowadays, my prayers for healing rarely last more than thirty seconds. I don't want to waste time in a long-winded prayer when I could be finding out what God has done.

If the person experiences some improvement, thank God, and pray again. If nothing appears to have changed, pray again. This is the only way to learn. When a person is not healed then and there, never say it's because they lack faith. This is not helpful. Whether healing happens or not, you'll want the person to experience the love of God for them through your ministry time.

Please don't be put off when nothing happens. You may pray for many people before you see the first one healed. Besides helping a person become a Jesus follower, few things will build your faith as much as seeing someone healed through prayer.

At times we get discouraged and want to stop praying for healing. When we do that, we stop learning, and no one gets healed.

Questions for Reflection and Conversation

1. Scripture is so important. Search through the Gospels and write down how Jesus prayed for healing. What patterns, if any, can you detect? How can you adjust your prayers to pray more like Jesus?

2. Have you found a good mentor? If so, how do you spend your time together? Or, if you mentor others,

how do you do this effectively? Share your experiences as a mentee or mentor with your group.

3. Do you know anyone who prays effectively for healing? If so, perhaps you could ask them if they would involve you in some of their prayers so that you could watch and learn. Maybe you'll be able to slipstream in their gifting to get a feel for this type of ministry.

4. Look for opportunities to pray for people to be healed. Keep them very low-key. You might simply say, "I know God heals people. Would you mind if I prayed with you? I know God loves you very much." Then pray a short, confident prayer. Call the person by name and thank God for them. Remember, even if the person is not healed, your prayer can still be powerful. God is always at work in mysterious ways.

FIVE

praying the course

"'In the last days, God says, I will pour out my
Spirit on all people. Your sons and daughters will
prophesy, your young men will see visions, your
old men will dream dreams.'"

—Acts 2:17

I don't play golf. I have no hand-eye coordination, and even
if I had, I don't see well enough to follow the little white
ball. Miniature golf is the best I can do. I know only one thing
about golf, other than you use a club to hit a ball toward a
hole. Or, in my crazy golf world, you use a club to hit the
ball through a tunnel, around a windmill, up a ramp, around
a curve, and finally into the hole. Regardless of whether you

are golfing at St. Andrews in Scotland or on a mini putt-putt course at a seaside resort, here's what I know: If you don't get out of the clubhouse, you can't play the first hole.

As simple as it is, I've found it quite an important spiritual concept. If God invites you to join with him in some ministry opportunity, it's like playing the first hole of a golf course. Each act of obedience and faith leads to the next, just as playing hole number one leads to hole number two.

You can choose to play or not to play. In golf, if you decide not to play, nothing will happen. In our followership of Jesus, we pray the holes instead of playing them. If we don't pray the first hole, we will miss the adventure of holes two, three, four, five, and so on. But, if you choose to follow God, you may be in for an adventure. One act of faith often leads to another opportunity.

Hole One: Darn Rugby Players

One day in 1986, I had a little nudge in my spirit that I should write out a brief testimony, have it printed, and pin it on every noticeboard at my university. I had forty notices printed and headed to the main building's sixth floor at Aston University to post them. I'd only pinned up two or three posters when a group of rugby players stopped to read the first poster. By now, I was near the other end of the corridor. I paused for a moment in case they had any questions. They didn't. Instead, they laughed and ripped the poster from the wall. The rugby players were the jocks of the campus, the influential students, the campus culture shapers. They made it abundantly clear what they thought about me and my story. The poster wasn't an invitation to a concert or an event; it was far more personal. It was my story. Their laughter and the aggressive way they ripped the poster down and tore it to pieces left me feeling humiliated.

I moved onto the next noticeboard to pin up my poster. The rugby players strolled up to the second noticeboard and ripped that poster down too. I turned the corner and moved to the next noticeboard. I was out of sight now. I hoped the rugby players had had their fun and would soon leave me alone. They didn't. I heard them loudly ripping my poster from the third noticeboard and slowly tearing it to pieces again. I moved further down the corridor; the rugby players turned the corner and walked up to the next noticeboard to repeat their shenanigans.

I wondered if I should stop posting the notices and come back another time, but I had the strongest impression I should continue. I pinned up several more posters, only to see several more pulled down. I was not only embarrassed; I was frustrated too. I'd spent considerable time, and quite a bit of money printing the posters, and no one other than the rugby players had had the opportunity to read them. To be honest, I was angry at God too. Why did he want me to keep going? Why couldn't I come back another time?

In my frustration, I prayed, "God, I don't understand. Why do I need to do this?"

I felt, rather than heard, his reply: "You will. Because you have obeyed me in such a small thing, I will send you as a prophet to the nations." It was a ridiculous idea. I'd only been out of England once in my life on a school trip to Northern Germany. Nonetheless, I hid the thought in my heart.

After tearing down a few more posters, the rugby players got bored or hungry and moved on. I continued pinning posters on the sixth floor and then walked down to the fifth, fourth, third, second, first, and ground floors.

Hole Two: Sarah

Very late that night, there was a knock on our apartment door. That was not unusual. I lived with a group of Malaysian guys who often had friends visit for nightlong games of mah-jongg. The clickety-clack-clack of the bamboo tiles on our kitchen table often woke me up. I didn't get up to answer the door; it was most unusual for me to have midnight callers. One of my Malaysian friends banged on the door and told me I had a visitor. I went to the apartment door, and there stood a slightly disheveled female undergraduate student. She introduced herself as Sarah, told me she'd read my poster, and wanted to learn about Jesus. I led her to the kitchen, and we talked for perhaps ten minutes. As she was leaving, I told her I'd connect her with a female friend of mine for follow-up.

A couple of days later, I introduced Sarah to Bev, one of my friends. I joined them for coffee with the intent of leaving them alone to talk. During our conversation, Sarah kept wincing in pain. My friend asked her what was wrong, and Sarah told us she had some stomach problems. I offered to pray with her. After coffee, the three of us found an empty room in the Student Union to pray. I simply asked Jesus to heal her. To my surprise, the power of God overwhelmed her, and she fell to the floor. None of us had expected that. I wasn't sure what to do next. It seemed apparent something good was happening. From what I'd already observed, Sarah was highly strung. She appeared stressed and anxious much of the time. Now, lying on the floor, Sarah was peaceful for the first time since I'd met her. After a few minutes, she got up from the floor and left with Bev to talk.

Hole Three: Yasmin

A week or so later, I was almost finished with lunch in the Student Union when Sarah approached my table with another girl in tow. "Can we talk to you?" she asked. I agreed, finished my lunch, and walked downstairs to meet them. We found a vacant room. Yasmin introduced herself and told me something about her story. Her extended family was from East Asia and now lived in Birmingham. She had recently become a Jesus follower to the dismay of her family.

Sarah interrupted, "Tell him about your pain."

Yasmin paused for a minute and then told us she suffered from severe stomach pains too.

"Pray for her like you prayed for me," insisted Sarah.

"Sure," I said. "I can certainly ask Jesus, but I don't have any special powers, so we'll have to leave the results to him."

"Jesus," I prayed. "Please heal Yasmin's stomach just like you did Sarah's."

As I prayed, Yasmin responded in much the same way as Sarah. Yasmin fell toward the floor. Between the two of us, Sarah and I just caught Yasmin before she hit the floor. Once again, it was evident the Holy Spirit was working in her life. A deep peace came upon her, her breathing deepened and slowed, and her body began to tremble. We left her lying on the floor for a few minutes and then helped her up. I asked her to let me know if her stomach condition improved.

Hole Four: Sarah Again

The following Sunday evening, I was walking across campus. It had been raining all afternoon, and I was honestly glad to get out of my room for some exercise. As I passed by Sarah's apartment building, I had the strongest impression that I must immediately go up to Sarah's room and help her become a Jesus follower. I did just that. I found her room quickly and knocked on her door. When Sarah opened the door, I simply told her I felt the Holy Spirit had sent me. Sarah invited me in. "I knew you would come," she told me. I prayed with her and left to continue my walk. Just like that. Boom, boom, boom. I'd spent hours trying to persuade various friends to follow Jesus. This time, there was no need for persuasion. She was ready.

Hole Five: Yasmin's Mom

A few days later, I passed Sarah on the way to my apartment. She looked like a different woman. She no longer looked disheveled. She had ironed her clothes; her eyes looked brighter; she had a big smile on her face. I've found that when a person begins to understand the depth of God's love and forgiveness, no matter what they've done, they begin to see themselves differently. No longer can they see themselves as trash or valueless. Instead, they get a first glimpse of how God sees them, as precious, as beautiful, as a prince or princess. It was lovely to see this transformation happening in Sarah.

Sarah didn't comment much about her conversion experience, but she did tell me Yasmin was much better. Furthermore, Yasmin's mom now wanted me to pray for her. I didn't give it much thought and agreed before heading off to a meeting. A couple of days later, Sarah told me that Yasmin planned to bring her mom to campus to meet me. She wanted me to pray for her mom's healing. We agreed to meet in Yasmin's apartment; Sarah gave me the address and a time to meet.

I went to Yasmin's room at the agreed time and discovered Yasmin's mom spoke no English. She wore a very traditional burqa, albeit with no face covering. The room didn't have enough chairs for us to sit, so we stood in the middle of the room. I turned to Yasmin and asked her to ask her mother what was going on. Yasmin spoke to her mom in Urdu and translated her mom's answers back to me. She told me that her mother, who I guessed must be in her forties, kept bleeding for days after her monthly menstruations. I now felt completely out of my comfort zone. I was a single guy in a room full of women about to pray for a Muslim mother with gynecological problems. I suddenly had this thought: she must be desperate. She was a Muslim woman using her daughter to translate to an unmarried Christian man in a university apartment. The religious and cultural barriers she had to cross to talk to me must have been significant. Yasmin told me more. Her mom had been unwell for quite some time, and several trips to see her doctor had not resolved the issue.

I asked Yasmin to ask her mom if I could touch her mom's shoulder lightly as I prayed. She agreed. As I began to pray, I felt Yasmin and Sarah add their hands to mine.

"Jesus, thank you for Yasmin's mom. Thank you for loving her. Please begin your healing process and make her whole."

After praying this brief prayer, we waited. There was a beautiful presence of Jesus in the room. Yasmin's mom wobbled and simply toppled over backward. In hindsight, perhaps I should have expected this. I did not. The three of us caught her just in time and rested her gently on the carpet.

My follow-up prayer was very different.

"Lord," I said under my breath, "please don't let anyone come in the room."

It was an earnest prayer. The Holy Spirit was clearly ministering to Yasmin's mom. She looked very peaceful. Her breathing had deepened and slowed. However, an outsider might have drawn very different conclusions. It looked like a crime scene. I imagined how a police officer would describe the scene:

"Judge, when I entered the room, I saw this petite Muslim woman in her early to mid-forties lying out cold on the floor. The suspect, a white male in his early twenties, stood over her with a big grin on his face. He kept saying it wasn't him. A likely story! His accomplices, two females in their late teens, one white, one South Asian, verified the suspect's story, but we believe they may all be in on it together."

Thankfully, no one knocked on the door. Yasmin, Sarah, and I merely asked the Lord to continue his work. While we were praying, much to her surprise, Sarah quietly began praying in tongues. After a few more minutes of prayer, I asked Yasmin to help her mom sit up. We were not sure what God had done, other than ministered peace to her. Nonetheless, I always like to thank God when he is visibly moving to invite him to do even more.

We ended our time praying for Yasmin's mom by thanking Jesus for his love. I asked Yasmin to translate this for her mom,

knowing she was a Muslim. If she improved, I wanted her to
know that it was Jesus who healed her.

Hole Six: Yasmin's family

I didn't see either Yasmin or Sarah for the next couple of weeks.
When I next met Yasmin, she told me her mom's bleeding had
stopped, she felt much better, and that her mom and many
others in her family had come to believe in Jesus as a result of
her healing.

Isn't that amazing? One act of obedience to pray more
intentionally set off a chain reaction leading to some healings
and an Islamic family encountering Jesus.

Resting in the Spirit

I've reflected on this series of incidents many times. It would
have been very easy for me to miss that first little nudge to
post my testimony around the university. The nudge wasn't
marked with a helpful flag alerting me that obedience would
set off a chain reaction. It was just a little nudge that I reluctantly obeyed. We never know which act of obedience will
start a new chain. Next, I'm intrigued by how many gifts the
Holy Spirit livestreamed to do his work: healings, prophecy,
words of knowledge, and praying in tongues. Third, I find it
interesting that all three women rested in the Spirit during
our times of prayer. This does happen from time to time.
Nowadays, I usually invite people to sit if possible when I'm

praying for them. Seeing people resting in the Spirit can be quite frightening for visitors or passersby, so I like to keep things as natural and low-key as possible. Earlier in my ministry, I saw more people rest in the Spirit, but fewer people healed. It was a spectacular but ineffective ministry. Finally, I find it interesting that Sarah began praying in tongues before she'd ever heard about this spiritual gift. For some reason, praying in tongues has been controversial in the church. What a pity since it's such a valuable gift.

Illuminated Manuscript!

During my first two years as a Christian, I'd heard the Holy Spirit mentioned, but only in terms of someone being a good teacher or an anointed evangelist. I'd never heard anyone talk about the gifts of the Holy Spirit, much less seen anyone use them effectively. Like Sarah, I had never heard anyone pray in tongues. My encounter with the Holy Spirit was very much a surprise to me, just like it was for Sarah several years later.

I was sitting in Lincoln Cathedral, England, in 1982, waiting for a friend's confirmation service to begin. I arrived early and, for almost an hour, I was the only person sitting in this magnificent cathedral that could seat well more than a thousand. Everything about the cathedral's architecture reminded me that God was huge, and I was not. To take my mind off my growing sense of unease, I decided to continue my Bible reading. Earlier in the year, I began reading through the Bible for the first time. I flew through Genesis and Exodus, then struggled through Leviticus and Numbers. By the time I sat alone in Lincoln Cathedral, I had just finished Deuteronomy and begun the first chapter of Joshua.

I'd been a reader for most of my life. I'd read hundreds of books by then. Nothing in my experience prepared me for what happened next. I finished Joshua chapter 2, turned the page, and began to read. As I read, Joshua 3, verse 5 began to glow on the page. I'd never seen anything like it. It's the type of thing we might see in a sci-fi movie, but it was happening right there in front of me. I'd never read Joshua 3:5 before. I hadn't underlined it with a yellow marker pen. What I was seeing was not an unusually bright highlighter or a trick of the light. The verse appeared to glow in front of my eyes. It was as if a bright flashlight was being shone through the page from the other side, focusing solely on this one verse. Verses 4 and 6 looked normal. Verse 5, on the other hand, glowed.

I was both excited and terrified. If the architecture of Lincoln Cathedral wasn't unsettling enough, I now had to deal with a glowing verse. I'd heard some Christians talk about a Scripture verse "jumping off the page." I wondered if this was the experience about which they were talking.

I read Joshua 3:5 several times: "Joshua told the people, 'Consecrate yourselves, for tomorrow the LORD will do amazing things among you.'"

As I read the verse, I was convinced God had something special planned for the following day. I honestly don't remember much about the confirmation ceremony or our drive back to Birmingham that evening. All I could think about was what God might be planning for the next day.

When I woke the next morning, it seemed a rather ordinary day. There were no rainbows from heaven, no illuminated Scripture verses, no voices from God. I wondered if I had imagined the whole episode, while, at the same time, I was concerned that I might somehow miss what God had planned, in much the same way that I sometimes missed buses or trains. I spent some time in prayer. I waited quietly, hoping God might speak. I heard nothing. I looked at my watch. It was still only 9:30 a.m.

I looked at my watch every few minutes. Nothing happened. Nothing had occurred by 10:00 or 11:00 a.m. I honestly had no idea what God might be planning, so I didn't even know where I should be looking. Did God want to say something to me from Scripture, a book, a friend, or a telephone conversation? I simply had no idea.

Just before noon, I was in the kitchen, boiling a kettle to make a cup of tea, when I had the strongest image livestream through my head. This time the Holy Spirit showed me a movie clip of students from my university Bible study group. Earlier in the year, I had been asked to co-lead a university Bible study group with a more experienced leader. Each week, one of us would consult Bible concordances and commentaries to lead a discussion on the passage of Scripture we were studying that week. Typically, we began our Bible study group with some worship songs. Each group member would then take it in turns to read the Scripture passage we were studying, one verse at a time. Either the other leader or I would lead the discussion. Toward the end of our meeting, we would each share our prayer requests to pray for each other during the week. We finished the sessions in prayer.

In this livestream, however, our Bible study group members were not following this pattern at all. Instead, I saw every group member kneeling on the floor with their hands raised in worship and tears running down their faces. As I watched this movie clip play in my mind, I became aware of the Holy Spirit's presence. I guess the vision lasted for thirty seconds. Toward the end of the livestream, the word *renewal* was superimposed, much like headlines are superimposed over moving images on a TV news show.

Renewal

While I knew some secular uses of the word *renewal*, I had no idea how it related to following Jesus. All my housemates had gone to their respective homes for Easter break, so I could not ask for their input. I went into each of their rooms to see if any of them owned any books about *renewal*. I couldn't find one single book with renewal in the title. However, after spending the next hour consulting the index at the back of every book in the house, I collected several books that I borrowed over the Easter break. Over the next few days, I read them all. Each book discussed being filled with the Holy Spirit and spiritual gifts like prophecy, healing, and speaking in tongues to one extent or another. As I read, I became hungry for a deeper relationship with the Holy Spirit. I needed to be renewed.

After I'd finished reading the books, I decided to ask the Holy Spirit to fill me. I believed the promise of God to pour out his Spirit on all people. I believed God was a good Father who longed to give good gifts and, most of all, the Holy Spirit, to those who asked.

As soon as I decided to pray, I could not get a moment alone. The telephone rang, visitors came to the door, and friends called around. I simply could not find any time or space to pray. Eventually, I went upstairs to our bathroom, closed the toilet seat lid, making it an altar, and prayed, "Thank you, Father, for loving me. Please baptize me with your Holy Spirit."

I didn't know what to expect. Some of the books I read described a climactic experience in which tongues (new prayer languages) flowed from the person spontaneously. This certainly didn't happen to me. But as I waited, I experienced a growing but gentle sense of the Holy Spirit resting on me. I felt such peace. It was beautiful. I then said to the Lord, "I'm now going to start praying in tongues. I believe it's a gift you have for me, Lord. So, I'm just going to start speaking."

Praying in Tongues

I'd never heard anyone speaking in tongues, so I had no idea what to expect. But I simply stopped talking in English and began to worship God in this language that just came. I felt very peaceful, but I certainly didn't feel euphoric in any way. To be honest, I was a little disappointed. It felt bizarre hearing myself speak in a language I could not understand. *How could this possibly help me?* I wondered. I prayed in tongues for perhaps five minutes or so and then went downstairs to read more books.

It troubled me that I didn't feel anything when I spoke in tongues. I wished I had someone to ask, but I didn't. I simply knew no one who even talked about spiritual gifts. I was on my own. Even though I didn't feel anything when I prayed in tongues, I did notice some positive changes in me. I read Scripture more eagerly. I worshiped more passionately. I felt closer to Jesus. This change wasn't instant, but it was noticeable both to me and to others.

When I first read about praying in tongues, I imagined it would be an unknown language that would uncontrollably burst forth from within me. I know some have this experience, but it was not mine. Instead, I learned I could start and stop speaking in this strange language at will. Like a tap or faucet,

I could turn it on and off when I chose. In this respect, it was no different from any other language. To speak English, I had to open my mouth and speak. I could choose to talk or remain silent instead. Speaking in tongues was the same. I could speak loudly or softly. I noticed my language in tongues had structure, pauses, emphases, and intonations. The only difference was that I couldn't understand it.

Spiritual Workouts

I found the Bible had much to say about speaking in tongues. The apostle Paul wrote that speaking in tongues is not talking to people but speaking directly to God (see 1 Corinthians 14:2). Speaking in tongues has the same effect on your spirit as working out in the gym has on your body; it builds you up and strengthens you (see 1 Corinthians 14:4). Jude encourages us to "[build] yourselves up in your most holy faith and [pray] in the Holy Spirit" (1:20).

The idea of this strengthening is not to build you up so you can show off to others. That would be idolatry. It's to make you spiritually stronger to serve others better. In 1 Corinthians 13, Paul mentions that if love is not your motivation for speaking in tongues, it becomes just like a big drumroll in a 1970's rock concert—noisy, but ultimately irrelevant. Paul doesn't put it quite that well, but you get the point!

Paul also points out that when someone speaks in tongues, "no one understands them; they utter mysteries by the Spirit" (1 Cor. 14:2). While speaking in tongues might encourage the person who speaks, it's of no value to the other listeners unless someone can interpret what the Spirit is saying. Here's my rule: If you have faith to bring a message in tongues in a public setting, pray for the interpretation, too, if no one is present with the gift of interpretation of tongues. Tongues without interpretation are like raising your hand for a high five and being left hanging! High fives only work when two hands come together. In public settings, messages in tongues only work if there's also an interpretation. Notice the word is *interpretation* and not translation. The person interpreting will communicate the message's meaning in tongues, not translate the message word for word. Sometimes the interpretation will be longer than the message in tongues; at other times, it will be shorter. A difference in the length of the message in tongues and its interpretation does not necessarily invalidate either of them.

Paul talks about the value of praying in the Spirit, which he didn't understand, and praying with his understanding, presumably in his first language, which he understood perfectly (see 1 Corinthians 14:15). I've found this advice most helpful. During my times of private prayer, I typically pray for a person or situation in English first. I'm aware I have a limited understanding and don't always know how to pray. Therefore, I also pray in tongues, allowing the Holy Spirit to pray through me.

Chasing the Dragon

I found Jackie Pullinger's book *Chasing the Dragon* most instructive. Jackie was a twenty-year-old English woman that God called in 1966 to work as a missionary in Hong Kong's infamous Walled City. Every day, she'd walk through the narrow alleyways of the Walled City crammed with opium dens, prostitutes, and triad gang members. As she walked through the streets, she talked to one person after another about Jesus, but found no one interested in learning more.

One of Jackie's close friends recommended to Jackie that she pray in tongues for fifteen minutes each day as part of her daily devotions. Jackie took the advice. She admits she rarely felt anything when she prayed in tongues. However, as she continued to pray in tongues daily, she noticed the people she met on her walks were ready to hear about Jesus. Even more miraculously, many opium addicts were freed from their addictions and, when filled with the Spirit, they spoke in tongues. They were set free by prayer rather than through medication. Her success in helping drug addicts was recognized by the Hong Kong government, who donated land, allowing her to set up the first St. Stephen's Society center in Hong Kong. Since then, tens of thousands of addicts have been freed from their addictions through prayer at St. Stephen's Society centers in Hong Kong and several other Asian nations. If you think speaking in tongues is phony, talk to these addicts or the Hong Kong government.

Today, I pray in tongues under my breath for an hour or so each day. Praying in tongues is now such a part of my life that I no longer consciously think about it. It's like an idling car engine always ticking over in the background, ready to be revved up should the need arise. I pray in tongues when I'm listening to music, driving, going for a walk, or making the bed. I've found praying in tongues keeps me more sensitive to the livestreams of the Holy Spirit, so I'm ready to join him when he initiates a new adventure of faith. In this respect, I find it the most beneficial of all the spiritual gifts.

Being Filled with the Holy Spirit

I've seen people filled with the Holy Spirit in many ways. The test in my mind is not how emotional or dramatic the experience, but whether lasting change occurs as a result. One of the most significant barriers for us to receive more of the Holy Spirit is that we expect a significant emotional experience. I've had many such times, and they are lovely. However, I've also had many moments when it's obvious the Holy Spirit is working powerfully in and through me when I feel nothing unusual. It's important to remember that we are asking to be filled with the Holy Spirit, not with something we can physically handle, taste, or touch. We may respond physically or emotionally when the Holy Spirit moves powerfully on us, often because some form of deep healing or release happens when the Spirit comes. However, it's important to remember that everything we receive from God, we receive by faith, not through feelings.

In Galatians 3:2–6, Paul asks the Galatian Christians the following:

> Did you receive the Spirit by the works of the law, or by believing what you heard? Are you so foolish? After beginning by means of the Spirit, are you now trying to finish by means of the flesh? Have you experienced so much in vain—if it was in vain? So again I ask, does God give you his Spirit and work miracles among you by the works of the law, or by your believing what you heard? So also Abraham "believed God, and it was credited to him as righteousness."

We receive the Holy Spirit by believing the truths we have heard. We have a good, good Father who is more than willing to give the Holy Spirit to those who ask him.

Over to You: Inviting the Spirit to Fill You

The first step is simply to ask God to fill you with the Holy Spirit. You can do this alone in your room, in a church, or in a small group with other Jesus followers. Perhaps you know someone who prays in tongues or livestreams other gifts you could invite to pray with you or your small group. If you already livestream, maybe you'll be the one asked to assist others. What a privilege.

When I am praying with people to be filled with the Holy Spirit, I often begin by reading Luke 11, especially verse 13. I want to remind people how much God longs to give them the gift of his Spirit. I then ask them to pray. In Luke 11:13, the Scripture says that "how much more will your Father in heaven give the Holy Spirit to those who ask him!" Personally asking God is an essential part of the receiving process. The prayer doesn't have to be lengthy or complicated. "Lord, please fill me with your Holy Spirit" is enough.

I encourage you to do both now. Read Luke 11 slowly, from verse 1 through verse 13. The context is important. Jesus is responding to the request: "Teach us to pray." Jesus' teaching goes much further than what we typically refer to as the Lord's Prayer. Jesus didn't stop with "lead us not into temptation," but talked about persistence in prayer; the importance of asking, seeking, and knocking; and the desire of the Father to give the Holy Spirit to those who ask him. Think about it this way: when the disciples asked Jesus to teach them to pray, he responded by telling them to ask the Father for the gift of the Holy Spirit.

Once you've read through the first thirteen verses of Luke 11, put down your things, quiet yourself, and simply invite the Holy Spirit to fill you for the first time or the thousandth time. I always encourage people to pray vocally rather than in their heads. Praying out loud nails our colors to the mast and reminds ourselves we are all in.

After the person has prayed out loud, I also ask the Holy Spirit to fill the person. I always like to include the person's name in my prayers so that they hear their names spoken before God. I might say, "Come, Holy Spirit, and fill Dermot with your love and power." I then wait. Sometimes people weep, sometimes they laugh, sometimes they speak in tongues, and sometimes they feel nothing at all. I ask the person to thank the Lord for filling them and encourage them to begin praying in tongues.

Praying in Tongues

Once I've prayed with folk to receive a more profound experience of the Holy Spirit, I like to encourage them to pray in tongues if this is something they desire. It's such a practical gift, and I think the easiest to receive. However, I believe it's not useful to insist someone pray in tongues. A gift forced upon us is no gift at all!

I recently prayed with a friend who struggled to begin speaking in tongues. This is not uncommon. I think some people expect the Holy Spirit to take over their tongues and force them to start talking. Occasionally, this does seem to happen, but I don't think it's the norm. Usually, we begin to speak ourselves, just not in English. That's often difficult for us Westerners to do. Initially, speaking in tongues can be very humbling; we must trust God that our words are significant to him. Praying in tongues is, therefore, always an act of faith.

Sometimes people get very self-conscious about the thought of praying in tongues. I can understand this. I can clearly remember how self-conscious I was the first time I heard an audio recording of me speaking in English. My voice sounded so different on the playback to how I heard it inside my head. I kept asking my parents if I really sounded like that; they assured me that I did. In much the same way, I felt very self-conscious when I began to speak in tongues. I was not used to hearing myself saying words I did not understand. If this is your experience, know that you're not alone, and you'll get over it.

Many people start to speak in tongues very quickly, but not all. When people struggle, it's essential never to force them to speak in tongues. However, I've found simple encouragement has helped several. If a person struggles to pray in tongues, I quietly pray in tongues beside them. Sometimes the very act of listening to someone else pray in the language the Holy Spirit has given to them is all the person seeking the gift needs to receive their prayer language.

At other times, I'll ask a person to pray about a specific matter in English. Just as they are getting into a flow in their prayer, I interrupt them and ask them to continue to pray for the same issue, but no longer in English. "Don't try to think up words," I tell them. "Just pray out the words that will come to your lips." When we pray for someone or something passionately, it's like building a spiritual head of steam. When a person can't release this spiritual pressure by praying in English, they will often begin speaking in tongues to complete the prayer.

This was exactly how it happened with our friend Megan. She recalls that when I told her to pray, only not in English, she somewhat mischievously thought, *Fine. I'll pray in Greek.* She managed to speak out about three or four words in Greek before she'd exhausted her knowledge and then started praying in tongues.

Over to You: The King's Speech

Quite recently, I discovered another helpful technique you could easily replicate. I was praying with Christie, one of Kathie's close friends. I asked her what she was hoping to receive from our time of prayer. She told us she'd like to begin praying in tongues. As I was praying for her, the Holy Spirit brought a scene from the movie *The King's Speech* to my mind. The film focuses on the future King George VI's attempts to overcome his stutter so that he was ready to address the nation when he became king. In this scene, Lionel Logue, the future king's Australian speech and language therapist, put headphones over King George's ears and played music so loudly that King George could no longer hear his voice. Remarkably, King George's stutter largely disappeared when he was no longer distracted by hearing his stuttering voice.

I thought I'd try this technique on Christie. I asked her to pop in her earphones, take out her iPhone, and play her favorite worship songs. Before hitting play, I asked her to worship God but told her she couldn't do it in English. I told her nothing was going to happen until she started to speak. If she'd take that first step of faith, her prayer language would naturally begin. That's what happened. She pressed play, nodded her head a few times to the beat, and started to worship in tongues. It took about twenty seconds. She was not distracted by hearing her voice. Once she'd got into a flow of praying in tongues, she took the earphones out to listen to herself speak. It was awesome!

Not long after Christie left our house to drive home, she sent Kathie a text saying, "I prayed in tongues all the way home."

She sent another text the following morning, saying, "I'm walking the dog and praying in tongues. It's like I can turn it off and on."

Praying in tongues has now become a regular part of Christie's life. She is praying the King's speech now!

If you'd like to begin praying in tongues, why not close the door, pop in your headphones, and listen to some of your favorite worship music? Ask God to give you the ability to worship in tongues and then begin to speak. Nothing will happen until you open your mouth, but I pray it won't be too long before you are praying the King's speech too!

Questions for Reflection and Conversation

1. Has one act of obedience in your life ever led to a chain reaction series of events? Think back over your life and see if you can spot an act of obedience that made the next opportunity possible. Does the possibility of starting a chain reaction change how you think about small acts of obedience, even when you don't understand what the Lord is doing?

2. Have you ever had experiences like my experience with Sarah when it was clear the Holy Spirit was leading you? What did you do? What happened as a result? Share your experiences with your group.

3. Have you ever wanted to pray in tongues? What has encouraged you or put you off seeking this gift?

4. If you regularly pray in tongues, when and where do you most often pray? In what ways have you found this gift helpful?

SIX

holy wind

"The wind blows wherever it pleases. You hear its sound, but you cannot tell where it comes from or where it is going. So it is with everyone born of the Spirit."

—John 3:8

R ose opened the door, took one look at me, and burst into tears.

Now I know I'm no Brad Pitt, but even I thought her reaction a little extreme!

During my first few months as a Jesus follower, I tried to persuade my friends to follow Jesus. I knew how powerfully Jesus had changed my life; I wanted my friends to meet him too. One by one, I told my friends about Jesus and offered to lend each of them my copy of *The Cross and the Switchblade*, the most influential book in my own salvation experience. I had no takers until Rose asked to borrow the book. I lent her my copy, said goodbye, and caught the train to begin my freshman year at Aston University.

I'd honestly forgotten that I'd given Rose the book until an impromptu midterm visit to see my parents. I arrived late one evening, and the next day, as I walked into the town center, I remembered I'd lent Rose the book. Rose's house was not on my regular walk home, but I decided to take a longer route to pass by her house in case she was there. I wanted to reread the book myself and lend it to some university friends.

I didn't know that Rose had picked up *The Cross and the Switchblade* to continue her reading on this same morning. The book tells Rev. David Wilkerson's captivating story. Wilkerson was a skinny preacher from rural Pennsylvania called by God to help violent teenage gang members and drug addicts in New York City. In her reading that morning, Rose read the account of one of Wilkerson's visits to New York City, this time as his wife was nearing the end of her pregnancy with their third child. During his visit, Wilkerson spent time telling Jo-Jo, a homeless, teenage gang member, about Jesus' love for him. Jo-Jo was skeptical; no one loved him. He asked Wilkerson if he wanted his new baby to be a boy or a girl. Wilkerson admitted he hoped for a boy as they already had two daughters. Jo-Jo prayed his first prayer, a simple prayer that if God loved him, a homeless boy from New York City, then let God prove his love by giving Wilkerson a son. Wilkerson admitted he felt cornered by Jo-Jo's "if-then" prayer and spent all night praying for his wife and this lost teenage boy. At 2:30 a.m. the following morning, Wilkerson's baby boy was born. Jo-Jo believed God had answered his prayer and became a follower of Jesus.

As Rose read Jo-Jo's story, she began to cry. "God, if you're real and you love me," she prayed, "then let Ivan call to my door today." She prayed her own if-then prayer. It was a ridiculous prayer. I only decided to visit my parents at the last minute. She had no way of knowing I was even in town.

An hour after she'd prayed her if-then prayer, I knocked on her door. Rose opened the door and burst into tears. Through her sobs, Rose signaled for me to go through to her kitchen. She wept uncontrollably for several minutes. I had no idea what was going on. I thought maybe a friend had died or she had split up with her boyfriend. She was so upset. Rose excused herself for a few moments. When she returned, she told me about her prayer and her utter shock when I called to her door. I was very excited for Rose and told her how much God loved her. I told her how Jesus was changing my life. I forewarned her that following Jesus could be costly. She was virtually living with her boyfriend at that time, and this was unwelcome news.

It was clear to me that God was working. After talking for an hour, I asked Rose if she wanted to become a Jesus follower. I was sure she would, but I was wrong. She was silent for a couple of minutes and then quietly said, "No, I can't. I love my boyfriend too much."

I left her house feeling very disappointed. It was clear to me that God had somehow led me to Rose's door. I also knew that God had a much better plan for her life. Yet, she decided against becoming a Jesus follower because she feared losing her boyfriend, a relationship that, as it turned out, only lasted a few more weeks.

The Invisible Hand

I've reflected on this incident for many years. First, my last-minute decision to return home, and my thought to visit Rose were like any other thoughts. Even though *The Cross and the Switchblade* spoke at length about the leading of the Holy Spirit, it never dawned on me that my thought to visit Rose might in any way be providential. These thoughts were so ordinary, so matter-of-fact. I'd imagined that if God ever spoke directly to me, it would sound dramatic and booming. I had a lot to learn. I certainly didn't get a sense that I was compelled to visit Rose in any way whatsoever. I was thoroughly in control of my actions, yet God had led me without me even knowing it. It was only when Rose opened her door, burst into tears, and told me her story that I had my first inkling the Holy Spirit was at work.

Second, I was also surprised God answered Rose's if-then prayer. To me, these seem like manipulative prayers, and certainly not prayers I've ever seen God rushing to answer. Clearly, God hadn't changed the gender of Wilkerson's baby in answer to Jo-Jo's if-then prayer. Nonetheless, the prayer changed Jo-Jo's life. God's answer to Rose's prayer was far more statistically improbable. After all, Jo-Jo had a fifty-fifty shot of guessing the right gender of Wilkerson's baby. In contrast, the chances of my turning up unannounced on Rose's doorstep on the exact day she prayed must be a zillion to one. It was like an invisible hand was bringing all the parts together. Even more puzzling was that Rose clearly knew that God was at work, but still decided not to become a Jesus follower at that point in her life. As best as I could, I had spelled out that following Jesus could be costly. At least she was honest enough to know she was unwilling to pay that cost right then.

Finally, I wrote down everything that had happened that day so that I had a written record. I've found it helpful to keep a pen and notebook handy, so you can record what the Lord says and does. A journal gives us a permanent record that we can refer to in the days to come. Additionally, the very act of writing sometimes draws our attention to aspects of God's work we'd overlooked during the livestream.

Keeping the Record Straight

I've learned a written record is a powerful tool during times of discouragement. Just as the serpent tempted Eve with the question: "Did God really say?" (Gen. 3:1), during times of discouragement, he may whisper to you: "Did God really do that?" If you've recorded what God has done, you can look it up repeatedly and use it as a weapon in your spiritual warfare. Jesus gives us a clue into some of Satan's strategies when he tells us, "The thief comes only to steal and kill and destroy" (John 10:10). Recording what God has done with pen and paper puts a spiritual burglar alarm on our memories, helping to keep them safe from the thief. When we reread our notes and remember God's greatness, we switch on the alarm.

I can't overstate the value of keeping a journal. One of Satan's strategies is to convince us that we are less than we are. He wants to replace God's truths about us, that we are sons and daughters of the King, more than conquerors, and dearly loved by our heavenly Father, with demonic lies whispering that we are failures, inept, and bedraggled. If we take the bait, swallowing these lies hook, line, and sinker, our confidence to livestream the Spirit's gifts will shatter. When this happens, we tend to pass over an increasing number of opportunities the Lord gives to partner with him out of fear and rejection. No matter how enticing the devil presents his lies, all fragranced and wrapped up in cute little packages, they all contain incendiary devices aimed at maiming us spiritually, emotionally, relationally, and sometimes physically too. It's no wonder that Scripture is so insistent that we resist the devil.

The Invisible God

I often wonder what became of Rose. I pray for her from time to time as the Holy Spirit brings her to my mind. Her story reminds me of how difficult it is to follow an invisible God. She could see her boyfriend, hold his hand, and talk with him over dinner. If we follow God with any intentionality, we must learn to trust a God we cannot see and whose hands we can't physically hold. And he's not satisfied when we only trust him a little; he wants us to believe him for everything: our work, our dreams, our finances, and our very lives. He even wants us to trust him when things don't turn out as we had hoped or planned.

The human temptation is to fill this sensory vacuum with something else. When Moses met with God high up on Mount Sinai, the Israelites, newly escaped from Egypt, were melting down their gold jewelry to cast an idol, the infamous golden calf. We face the same temptation. We can't see God, and the constant temptation is to fill our sensory void with material things, whether they be church activities, music, shopping, sports, or video games. I find it intriguing that the apostle John ends his first epistle with this exhortation: "Dear children, keep yourselves from idols" (1 John 5:21).

John knew how strong and subtle the temptations are to replace our trust in the invisible God with more tangible things and warned us that creating any form of idol robs us of intimacy with God.

Wonderfully, Jesus hasn't left us all alone. In John 16:7, Jesus tells his followers (including us) that it is for our benefit that he went back to the Father; that was the only way we could experience the Holy Spirit in new and beautiful ways. Of course, we can't see the Holy Spirit with our physical eyes either, but we can at least train ourselves to see where the Spirit is moving and live our lives in such a way that we continually invite him to come close.

Where the Wind Blows

The Hebrew word for spirit is *ruach*, which means "breath" or "wind." While we can't see wind, we can at least see its effects: leaves blowing along the ground, a kite flying in the air, or the scattered debris following a tornado, typhoon, or hurricane.

In his conversation with Nicodemus, Jesus tells him, "The wind blows wherever it pleases. You hear its sound, but you cannot tell where it comes from or where it is going. So it is with everyone born of the Spirit" (John 3:8).

What an intriguing statement: "The wind blows wherever it pleases. . . . So it is with everyone born of the Spirit." Had Nicodemus visited Jesus during the daytime in one of the towns around the Sea of Galilee instead of in Jerusalem, where this encounter likely occurred, I wonder if Jesus would have pointed to one of the fishing boats bobbing up and down on the sea and said to Nicodemus, "Look at those boats, Nicodemus. Those fishermen have no idea where the wind is coming from or where it is going. One minute there's only a gentle breeze; the next, the winds roar in from another direction. But look, no matter the wind's strength or direction, you can see the fisherman doing the same thing: they hoist their sails so that the wind blows them along. Nicodemus, everyone born of the Spirit hoists their sails so that they can catch the wind. That's the only way you can live by the Spirit."

Jesus says that those full of the Spirit are swept along by this wind, never quite sure where they are heading, trusting the Holy Spirit will take them where God wants them to go. This was undoubtedly the apostle Paul's experience. In Acts 16:6–10, we see Paul preaching in what is now Turkey, obviously intent on heading east into Asia.

> Paul and his companions traveled throughout the region of Phrygia and Galatia, having been kept by the Holy Spirit from preaching the word in the province of Asia. When they came to the border of Mysia, they tried to enter Bithynia, but the Spirit of Jesus would not allow them to. So they passed by Mysia and went down to Troas. During the night Paul had a vision of a man of

Macedonia standing and begging him, "Come over to
Macedonia and help us." After Paul had seen the vision,
we got ready at once to leave for Macedonia, concluding
that God had called us to preach the gospel to them.

As we can see in Acts 16:6, the Holy Spirit kept them "from
preaching the word in the province of Asia," and in verse 7,
we read, "they tried to enter Bithynia, but the Spirit of Jesus
would not allow them to." We are left guessing how or why
the Holy Spirit blocked their paths, but whatever happened,
Paul attributed it to the work of the Holy Spirit. Furthermore,
in verse 9, we see the Holy Spirit redirecting Paul, this time
through a vision of "a man of Macedonia." Notice Paul's
response: "we got ready at once . . . concluding that God had
called us to preach the gospel to them." Paul immediately
changed plans to follow the Holy Spirit's lead to Europe. Paul
was like a kite, never sure where the wind would take him, but
always seeking to be blown along to wherever the Lord wanted
him to minister.

Paul had learned to trust the Holy Spirit. If he had not, I'm
sure many times he would have run in the opposite direction.
Acts 21:10–14 is a good example. Here, the prophet Agabus
comes down from Judea to meet Paul. He takes Paul's belt and
ties it around his own wrists saying, "In this way the Jewish
leaders in Jerusalem will bind the owner of this belt and will
hand him over to the Gentiles" (v. 11).

Hearing this, his companions pleaded with Paul not to continue his journey to Jerusalem. Paul was not dissuaded and responded, "Why are you weeping and breaking my heart? I am ready not only to be bound, but also to die in Jerusalem for the name of the Lord Jesus" (v. 13).

The Upper Room

Paul trusted the Spirit's leading, even when the path ahead was life-threatening. Paul's focus was not on himself, not even on the church, but on obeying and bringing glory to God. I've seen this type of resoluteness to serve God several times throughout my life. For example, in the early 2000s, I had the privilege of speaking to a group of young church leaders in an Asian nation where Christians experience constant persecution. When I arrived in this country, I naively asked my host, Ms. Anderson, to collect me from the hotel. She winced.

"We can't meet at the hotel," she explained, "in case we are followed."

I didn't like the sound of that.

"Do you have a map?" she asked.

I nodded and pulled out the map I'd picked up from the hotel reception. Ms. Anderson studied the map, circled my hotel, and stabbed an intersection four of five blocks away with her sharpened pencil.

"We'll meet you here," she said, pointing to the hole she'd just made in my map. "Be there at eight o'clock tomorrow evening. Stand in the doorway of the first shop on the street. It'll be closed by then, so no one will bother you. Some friends will park right outside at 8:00 p.m. in a red truck. You'll get in the back."

Ms. Anderson added that I should wear jeans and a dark sweater or shirt.

"The room will be quite warm, so try not to wear anything too thick," she advised.

The next evening, I left the hotel and walked to the rendezvous point. It was just starting to get dark, but the streets were well lit. I found the shop on a relatively quiet road and waited. The red truck pulled up at eight o'clock on the dot, and I hopped in the back. There were two men in the truck, a driver and a passenger.

"Anderson, she meet us there," the driver told me in somewhat broken English. His companion handed me a black wooly hat. "Put on. Cover hair." I soon learned that my blonde hair quickly set me apart as a foreigner, even at night.

The truck rattled and bumped its way through the streets. I guess we traveled for forty minutes or so. While the city center was well lit, I noticed fewer streetlights the longer we drove. Eventually, we arrived at a tall apartment building. Even in the darkness, it was apparent this was not an affluent neighborhood.

I started to open my door to get out.

"Wait," the driver whispered. "Not time yet."

We sat for ten minutes or so in silence. I was looking up at the dimly lit apartments when all the lights suddenly went out.

"Time," the driver whispered. We got out.

I couldn't see anything; it was pitch black. One of the men took hold of my arm and led me to a door. The man took my hand and placed it on an iron stair rail, and we began to climb one flight of stairs after another. The iron railing was cold and dusty. After many flights of stairs, I was led to a door and into a candlelit room. I heard the door close and, as if by magic, the apartment building's lights came back on.

Including me, there were twenty-one in the room: sixteen young church leaders, Ms. Anderson, a translator, and the two men from the truck. When Ms. Anderson had asked me to lead this leadership training segment, I imagined the leaders would be in their thirties or forties, perhaps older. I was wrong. One of these church leaders was only eighteen, although she looked much younger. All but one, I learned, were under twenty-five.

The evening began with a simple meal of vegetables and noodles and some tea. There were no chairs in the room. Ms. Anderson sat on the floor next to me and briefed me.

"The eight girls sleep in this room, and the eight guys sleep in a similar room next door. We meet in this room as it's a little tidier. All the leaders eat, study, and pray together. They just sleep in different rooms. The church is growing so fast that leaders are getting younger and younger."

She pointed to a young woman. To my Western eyes, she looked about fourteen but was, in fact, twenty-two.

"She leads a church of over one thousand."

My jaw dropped.

"Most of them lead only small churches of several hundred to a few thousand."

Did she say, "small churches of several hundred to a few thousand?" I felt like an imposter. The church I helped lead in Dublin ran just around one hundred members. What on earth could I teach these leaders?

After the noodle bowls and cups had been taken away, the meeting started. This time the interpreter sat next to me to explain what was going on.

The meeting began with singing. I was surprised. I'd imagined the group would not want to draw any attention to themselves, but they sang loud and long. There's no way the singing could have been heard from the street as we were too high up. However, the singing must have been heard in neighboring apartments and the apartments directly above or below. I asked the interpreter why they were singing so loudly. She shrugged her shoulders as if it were a stupid question. I never did get an answer.

She did, however, translate some of the words of the songs. Rather than the "I love you, Jesus" or "thank you for loving me" type of song lyrics I sang regularly in Dublin, these songs were all about honoring Jesus in difficult times, standing firm in persecution, and telling others about Jesus. As they sang their hearts out, I felt ashamed. I realized how little I knew of the struggle of the global church.

I was honestly hoping they would not ask me to speak. I needed to learn from these leaders, not them from me. But I was asked to speak. As soon as I began to talk, the Holy Spirit's presence came into the room powerfully. It felt like a warm blanket was resting on our shoulders. After my teaching, I moved into a time of prophetic ministry. I've forgotten all the prophetic messages I gave that evening except for one. That one I'll never forget.

As I moved from leader to leader, I rested my hand on each of their shoulders and prayed the words the Lord livestreamed to me. When I came to the oldest leader (I had learned he was almost thirty years old), the Lord gave me a word: "Tell him, 'You will be on the run from the authorities all your life because of your love for Jesus.'"

I began arguing with the Lord. "I can't tell him that," I said. "That's terrible. What if I'm wrong?" I like to give encouraging and comforting words. This prophetic word didn't seem encouraging at all. Nonetheless, obediently, I laid my hands on his shoulders and began to pray. By this time, I'd prayed over most of the other leaders in the room. Typically, they bowed their heads as I prayed. This leader didn't. He lifted his head and looked me straight in the eyes. This made it so much harder to speak the message.

As I looked him in the eyes, I felt this deep compassion rising inside me.

"The Lord says to you, 'You will be on the run from the authorities all your life because of your love for Jesus.'"

As the translator began to translate the words, tears began to roll down my cheeks.

The young leader nodded. He said something to the translator, who, in turn, translated his words for me.

"That's the second time I've been given that word in the last few months."

In my heart, I was feeling sorry for him. He was going to suffer for following Jesus.

He turned and said the most extraordinary thing to the translator.

"What a privilege. What a privilege to suffer for Jesus," she translated.

I thought bringing a word about suffering for Jesus would be a real downer. This man, who loved Jesus so profoundly, counted it an honor and a privilege. He had learned to trust Jesus more deeply than me. It was a humbling, holy moment. I'll never forget his response or his love for Jesus. I can no longer read Acts 5:41 without thinking of this man: "The apostles left the Sanhedrin, rejoicing because they had been counted worthy of suffering disgrace for the Name."

I was back the following night for the second half of my training. Around 11:00 p.m., just as we were finishing off our goodbyes, an audible gasp went around the room. A visitor had slipped into the meeting. Everyone went to greet him. While I was waiting to be introduced, the translator told me the man was regarded as an apostle in this nation.

"He oversees thousands of churches. We hardly ever see him. We certainly didn't expect him to come today. None of us know his real name. He has seven aliases, but we only know one. He uses the aliases to avoid the police who want to arrest him for speaking about Jesus."

When I shook his hand, I felt the overwhelming love of Christ to an extent I'd never experienced before or since. This man, whoever he was, simply glowed with the love of Christ. He thanked me for coming. He thanked *me!* It should have been me thanking him for the privilege of serving these brothers and sisters.

A couple of months later, I heard from Ms. Anderson that the local police had raided this leadership training camp a week or so after I was there. The police arrested several of these young church leaders, although some avoided capture. Despite this constant persecution, or perhaps because of it, this Asian country is seeing a great awakening.

I met these young Asian Christian leaders almost twenty years ago, and their witness still impacts my life. I've had the privilege of seeing the Holy Spirit work powerfully around the world. However, I've never experienced the Holy Spirit's power as I did those two nights in that small apartment building, high above an Asian street. As far as I know, there were no healings, no prophetic words other than the ones I brought, no words of knowledge. I simply met Jesus there, living in these young men and women.

I went into those meetings with a focus on helping those Asian church leaders lead their congregations well. I left the meetings with a passion for awakening. Imagine being in a situation where so many people begin to follow Jesus that eighteen-year-olds must pastor churches of several hundred new believers. Come, Holy Spirit.

Spiritual Isobars

In Jesus' time, the wind, like so many natural phenomena, was a mystery. People didn't know where the wind came from or where it was going. We know far more today. I'm sure you must have seen a meteorologist on television forecasting the weather in your region. If you have, you've likely seen isobars on a weather map. The isobars are the lines that connect areas of equal atmospheric pressure. Sometimes the weather announcer will highlight high-pressure areas; at other times, they might identify low-pressure regions. Whether the forecast is rain or shine, one thing remains constant: winds always blow from high pressure to low pressure. All we need to do to get the wind to blow our way is to create a low-pressure zone.

I like to think about the Holy Spirit's wind in the same way, and I often picture spiritual isobars. If wind always moves from high pressure to low pressure, all we need to do is create a low-pressure zone's spiritual equivalent.

During the 2008 Beijing Summer Olympics, the Chinese government reportedly invested millions in weather modification systems to prevent rain from disrupting the summer games. In 2009, the Beijing Weather Modification Office created a snowstorm. Here's the question: If governments can influence natural weather patterns, can Jesus followers create the conditions to attract a move of the Holy Spirit, a great awakening?

I believe the answer is yes and no. The timings of great moves of the Spirit ultimately lie in God's hands alone. Acknowledging that, I believe Scripture gives us several ways to create spiritual low-pressure zones that attract the Holy Spirit's wind. James 4:4–10 gives us examples of actions we can take that create areas of low pressure on our spiritual isobar chart, causing the Holy Spirit to come close. The passage also reveals attitudes and activities that repel the Holy Spirit:

> You adulterous people, don't you know that friendship with the world means enmity against God? Therefore, anyone who chooses to be a friend of the world becomes an enemy of God. Or do you think Scripture says without reason that he jealously longs for the spirit he has caused to dwell in us? But he gives us more grace. That is why Scripture says: "God opposes the proud but shows favor to the humble."

> Submit yourselves, then, to God. Resist the devil, and he will flee from you. Come near to God, and he will come near to you. Wash your hands, you sinners, and purify your hearts, you double-minded. Grieve, mourn and wail. Change your laughter to mourning and your joy to gloom. Humble yourselves before the Lord, and he will lift you up.

James writes that humility, repentance, submission to God, and resisting the devil are mouthwatering to the Holy Spirit. In contrast, the Holy Spirit finds worldliness and pride repugnant; they repel the Holy Spirit's wind.

The young Asian leaders I met seemed to have learned these principles. They lived humbly, they submitted to one another, and they surrendered to the Lord. They stood up against evil and were quick to repent. When fertilized with prevailing prayer and intercession for their nation, these attitudes created a low-pressure zone that the Holy Spirit kept filling and filling again. The Spirit continues to blow across this nation. Come, Holy Spirit.

Late-Night Prayer Walk

I moved to San Diego for a year between July 2012 and June 2013 to work as the dean of the Fermanian Business School at Point Loma Nazarene University. Oh my, that is one gorgeous campus! My office overlooked the Pacific Ocean, and I would frequently get e-mails telling me where to see the whales or dolphins. The sunsets were spectacular and the students were first-class. Every residence hall had a surfboard rack and one residence hall was built on top of a cliff so that early-morning surfers would navigate a well-worn route down to the sea and catch some morning waves before class.

Just before the beginning of the fall semester, I was walking past Brown Chapel when I heard a student worship band practice. I just stood outside and worshiped. The presence of the Holy Spirit just outside the chapel was glorious, and the band was only practicing. What would it be like when students, faculty, and staff filled Brown Chapel to worship? I couldn't wait.

I sent an e-mail to George Williamson, Point Loma's director of worship ministries. He led the band rehearsal, and I told him how much I appreciated his sensitivity to the Holy Spirit. We met for coffee and became friends. George is delightful. He is an accomplished musician who is generous with his time in meeting with and mentoring students. There is much he could boast about, but he lives a life of genuine humility.

Not long after our meeting, George asked if he could interview me in chapel. I readily agreed. I told a few of the stories in this book, and toward the end, gave a word of knowledge:

> There's a female student here that God wants to minister
> to this morning. I don't know who you are, but this is
> what I know about you. Just before you left your home

to come to Point Loma this semester, you argued with your mom; and this argument had something to do with your weight. Whatever was said, the conversation has strained your relationships with your mom, and God wants to heal the relationship. I'll hang around at the front of Brown Chapel for a while. I'd love to pray with you.

I had the opportunity to pray with several students who responded to the word of knowledge, and I thought the matter was closed.

The next day, a parent called me on my office phone:

Dr. Filby, I want to give you a heads-up about a conversation I've just had with my daughter, Mandy. She called me right after your chapel talk and was very upset. She was so angry and said, "Mom, how dare you call one of the university professors and tell them about our private conversation?"

I had no idea what she was talking about and assured her I had not contacted anyone at Point Loma. I asked her what was going on, and she told me about what you had said in chapel about the mom and daughter arguing about the daughter's weight. I told my daughter the Holy Spirit must be at work, and she should make an appointment to see you.

Dr. Filby, I don't know what she will tell you, but here's what we are concerned about: She was always a very outgoing young woman, but she changed entirely eighteen months ago. Instead of going out, she spent all her time in her room. She's put on lots of weight and looks unhealthy. We are concerned about her. We'd be grateful for anything you can do. We just want our daughter back.

I assured the mother I would willingly pray with Mandy if she contacted me, but she had to initiate that conversation. Mandy did call me later in the day, and we set up a time to meet in my office. Mandy shared with me that eighteen months ago one of her best friends died in a tragic accident and she had struggled with depression ever since. Mandy hated who she'd become. She felt trapped but unable to find a way out of depression.

I asked Mandy if I could pray with her and she agreed. God did a beautiful miracle in her life. God's power snapped whatever forces were binding her. Her countenance changed even as we prayed together. She became joyful. Jesus was setting her free; he's good at that.

Mandy's father flew down to San Diego to personally thank me for being sensitive to the Holy Spirit's prompting. Days don't get much better than that.

About a month after my chapel address, I was getting ready for bed one night. I'd already put on my pajamas and brushed my teeth. It was time to do some nighttime reading. Just as I picked up my book, I kept getting the strongest impression I needed to get up, walk around campus, and pray for the university. I was in bed about to read my book. I thought to myself, *I could just as easily walk around campus the next day.* The impression did not go away and became more insistent. I needed to walk around campus and pray that very night.

I put down my book, got dressed, and began my prayer walk. I walked from my apartment toward the Fermanian School of Business, praying for the students living in those apartments and the business school's work. I walked through campus, past the School of Education's laboratory school, praying for the young children educated there on campus. I walked down toward the president's office, praying for our students, President Bob Brower, faculty, and staff. I turned the corner and walked past Brown Chapel, praying for the university chaplains and George Williamson. As I walked past the dining commons, I saw nine students sitting in a circle on the ground. One of the students recognized me from chapel and called out to me.

"Dr. Filby, come over here a minute."

I walked over to the group.

"Did you feel it too?" one of the students asked.

"Did I feel what?"

I was in Southern California, smack bang in the middle of earthquake activity. I assumed I'd missed a small tremor.

"Were you in your room tonight and had the impression you needed to get up, walk around campus, and pray for the university?"

"Yes, I was. How do you know? Why do you ask?" I was sensing God was moving in another of his mysterious ways.

The student pointed to every student sitting in the circle.

"Each of us felt it too."

God had livestreamed to these students to walk around campus and pray for the university at the very same time. We chatted for a few minutes and moved to the prayer chapel to worship and pray together for another hour. We agreed to meet every week to continue our prayer for the university.

How does God do that? How does he tell ten people the same thing at the same time? I could have easily stayed in bed and read. If I had, I would have missed another opportunity to see God at work.

What if God is speaking now, not to ten people in San Diego, but millions of Jesus followers worldwide? What if he's not looking for single boats to sail solo, but for all our little boats to form vast flotillas, all blown in the same direction by the Holy Spirit's wind? What might happen if Jesus followers came together to pray without ceasing?

Over to You: Our Dunkirk Moment

Dunkirk was one of the most popular movies of 2017. Written, directed, and produced by Christopher Nolan, the war movie depicts the rescue of British and French troops cornered at Dunkirk by the advancing German troops. No one expected the British or French soldiers to survive; they faced overwhelming odds. The German Air force, the mighty Luftwaffe, was preparing to attack the stranded troops. The German army was moving in.

In British Naval Headquarters, below Dover Castle, Vice Admiral Bertram Ramsay hatched a plan to rescue, at most, thirty thousand men by sending destroyers and support vessels to Dunkirk to ferry them home. Simultaneously, King George VI (he of *The King's Speech* mentioned in chapter 5) called for a National Day of Prayer. Millions of people responded. One famous photograph shows hundreds of men and women lining up outside Westminster Abbey, waiting for their turn to enter and pray. Churches overflowed.

As the people prayed, a violent storm erupted over Dunkirk, grounding the Luftwaffe. Concurrently, a great calm settled on the typically stormy English Channel, enabling hundreds of small boats to join the destroyers to sail back and forth, back and forth, across the channel, saving lives. Ramsey hoped his plan would save 30,000 men. As it turned out, more than eight hundred boats helped save 338,000 men from death or capture. One headline in the British newspaper *The Sunday Mirror* from 2 June 1940, read: "Boy, 15, Brings Troops Home." It told the story of a fifteen-year-old boy and several seventeen-year-olds who volunteered in the rescue. The young and old all had a part to play.

I wonder if this could be our Dunkirk moment. What would happen if Jesus followers worldwide, from every denomination, came together to pray for the greatest awakening the world has yet seen? Together, could we change our spiritual weather patterns through repentance and prevailing prayer? Could we lower the spiritual isobars? Could we invite the Holy Spirit to blow on, in, and through us again for the world's sake?

Millions of men and women are trapped by the advancing troops of materialism, hedonism, and the culture of "anything goes." Whether they know it or not, Jesus Christ is their only hope.

It's time to hoist our sails. Whether you are fifteen or ninety-five, you have a vital part to pray. Lives are at stake. It's time for a great awakening. Are you ready?

Come, Holy Spirit.

Questions for Reflection and Conversation

1. Can you remember times when a person's name or face came to your mind during a time of prayer? What did you do? Did you ignore the thought, pray for the person, or reach out to contact them if that was possible? If you made contact, how did they respond? Share your experiences with your group.

2. Have you ever had experiences like my experience with Rose when it was clear the Holy Spirit was leading you, even though you were unaware? What happened? Share your experiences with your group.

3. Meditate on Acts 5:41. Have you ever thought it a privilege to be counted worthy to suffer shame for the name of Jesus?

4. Examine your life in the light of James 4:4–10. Are there things you can do and pray to change the spiritual isobars around you? Invite the Holy Spirit to blow in and through you for the sake of the world.

CPSIA information can be obtained
at www.ICGtesting.com
Printed in the USA
LVHW021034030921
696732LV00007B/13